A Legacy
OF VALOR

A Legacy OF VALOR

A History of Lifesaving and Shipwrecks at Montauk, New York

HENRY D. OSMERS

outskirts
press

The opinions expressed in this manuscript are solely the opinions of the author and do not represent the opinions or thoughts of the publisher. The author has represented and warranted full ownership and/or legal right to publish all the materials in this book.

A Legacy of Valor
A History of Lifesaving and Shipwrecks at Montauk, New York
All Rights Reserved.
Copyright © 2017 Henry D. Osmers
v3.0 r1.0

Cover Photo © 2017 Henry D. Osmers

This book may not be reproduced, transmitted, or stored in whole or in part by any means, including graphic, electronic, or mechanical without the express written consent of the publisher except in the case of brief quotations embodied in critical articles and reviews.

Outskirts Press, Inc.
http://www.outskirtspress.com

ISBN: 978-1-4787-7949-0

Outskirts Press and the "OP" logo are trademarks belonging to Outskirts Press, Inc.

PRINTED IN THE UNITED STATES OF AMERICA

For Betsy White (1940-2016)
For her great love of all things Montauk, and for her 30 years
of steadfast devotion to the Montauk Historical Society

Contents

Illustrations i
Acknowledgements v
Prologue ix

Chapter 1: General History of the U. S. Life Saving Service 1
Chapter 2: Montauk Point Life Saving Station 23
Chapter 3: Ditch Plain Life Saving Station 31
Chapter 4: Hither Plain Life Saving Station 51
Chapter 5: U. S. Coast Guard Station Montauk 69
Chapter 6: Notable Shipwrecks 1600s – 1877 77
Chapter 7: Notable Shipwrecks 1878 – 1914 99
Chapter 8: Notable Shipwrecks 1915 – 2000s 117
Chapter 9: Lost at Sea Memorial 145

Appendix A: Keepers/Officers in Charge of Montauk Life Saving and Coast Guard Stations 149
Appendix B: Lost at Sea Memorial Inscriptions 151

Bibliography 155
Endnotes 159
Index 167

Illustrations

1- The Life Line by Winslow Homer, 1884 vi
2- Montauk Point Lighthouse, 1871 vii
3- First House, Montauk xi
4- Second House, Montauk xi
5- Third House, Montauk xii
6- Alexander Hamilton 2
7- Sumner Increase Kimball 4
8- Lucretia Rudolph-Garfield 8
9- Joseph Francis 9
10- Francis surfboat 10
11- Beebe-McLellan surfboat 11
12- Self-righting Life Boat in action, ca.1879 11
13- Firing the Lyle Gun 12
14- Breeches Buoy 13
15- Breeches Buoy 13
16- Burning a Coston signal 15
17- Lifeboat headed for a ship in distress 16
18- A lifesaver on patrol 17
19- Henry E. Huntting, Superintendent of Long Island Life Saving Stations 19
20- Arthur Dominy, Superintendent of Long Island Life Saving Stations 20
21- Skeletal remains of a shipwreck at Montauk, ca. 1930 21
22- Chart of Montauk Point Lifeboat Station, 1880s 24
23- Jonathan A. Miller 25
24- Map of Montauk Point Light Station, 1890 26
25- Montauk Point Light Station, 1903 27
26- Boathouse at Montauk Point Lighthouse, ca. 1900 28
27- Montauk Point Lighthouse, pre-1910 29
28- Ditch Plain Life Saving Station, 1885 31
29- Inventory of Public Property, Ditch Plain Station, March 31, 1873 33
30- Chart showing location of Ditch Plain Coast Guard Station 35
31- Ditch Plain Life Saving Station, 1894 36
32- Ditch Plain Coast Guard Station, 1921 37
33- Coast Guard crew at Ditch Plain Coast Guard Station, 1941 38
34- Stationery items for Ditch Plain Life Saving Station, 1881 40

35- Supply request for Ditch Plain Life Saving Station, 1874...41
36- Frank D. Warner at Quogue Life Saving Station, 1905 42
37- Frank D. Warner at Ditch Plain Coast Guard Station, 1935 43
38- Articles of Engagement for Surfmen at Ditch Plain Station, December 1874 44
39- Travel expenses for drill and exercise, Ditch Plain Station, July 1873 45
40- Crew members at Ditch Plain Life Saving Station, 1893..47
41- Aerial view of Ditch Plain Coast Guard Station during World War II...48
42- Ditch Plain Coast Guard Station, August 16, 1941 49
43- Lookout Tower at Ditch Plain Coast Guard Station, August 16, 1941 49
44- Former Ditch Plain Coast Guard Station building, January 2016..50
45- Hither Plain Station as it appeared in 1934...52
46- Chart showing location of Hither Plain Coast Guard Station..53
47- Inventory of Public Property, Hither Plain Station, March 31, 1873 55
48- Isolation evident in view of Hither Plain Coast Guard Station..56
49- Dirigible floating by Hither Plain Coast Guard Station, ca. 1917 57
50- Hither Plain Coast Guard Station in the 1930s..58
51- Testing lifesaving equipment at Hither Plain Coast Guard Station..59
52- Articles of Engagement, Hither Plain Station, December 1874 61
53- Travel expenses for drill and exercise, Hither Plain Station, July 1873 62
54- Postcard view of Hither Plain Life Saving Station 63
55- Old Montauk Highway at Hither Plain Coast Guard Station, May 1924..64
56- Old Montauk Highway at Hither Plain Coast Guard Station, January 2016.....................................65
57- Signal flags flying at Hither Plain Coast Guard Station, 1919 66
58- Hither Plain Coast Guard Station during World War II..67
59- Napeague Coast Guard Station after the Hurricane of September 21, 1938...................................70
60- Napeague Coast Guard Station building prepared for move to Star Island in Lake Montauk, 1954 71
61- Napeague Coast Guard building en route to Star Island, Montauk, 1954.......................................72
62- Napeague Coast Guard building entering Lake Montauk, March 1955..73
63- Coast Guard Station Montauk, January 2016..75
64- *Culloden* in its sailing days 79
65- *Culloden* ship model at Montauk Point Lighthouse Museum..80
66- *Flying Cloud*...83
67- *John Milton* wreck site, 2008...86
68- *John Milton* monument, 2008...88
69- Bell from the *John Milton*, 2009 88
70- *Great Eastern* picking up trans-Atlantic cable, 1865 90
71- *Great Eastern* ship model at Montauk Point Lighthouse Museum...91
72- *Circassian*, December 1876...96
73- *Circassian* survivors struggle to the beach, December 1876..97
74- James Scott, keeper at Montauk Point Lighthouse 101
75- The schooner *Lewis King* aground at Montauk, 1887...102
76- Engineer's log for the *George Appold*, October 1888 105
77- The Clyde liner *Chippewa* aground at Montauk, July 1908 111
78- *Comanche II* aground at Montauk Lighthouse, 1935 121

ILLUSTRATIONS

79- *Comanche II* aground at Montauk Lighthouse, 1935 121
80- *Red Sail* on rocks at Montauk Point Lighthouse, 1946 127
81- Motorboat wrecked at Montauk Point, June 1, 1955 131
82- U.S.S. *Baldwin* being refloated off Montauk Point, June 1961 134
83- *Atlantic Cape* ashore at Fort Pond Bay, 1972 137
84- *Elizabeth R* ashore in Fort Pond Bay, 1979 140
85- Lost at Sea Memorial, Montauk Point Lighthouse, 2010 147
86- Lost at Sea Memorial, Montauk Point Lighthouse, 2015 148

Acknowledgements

OTHER THAN MY home computer, which served as my base of operations, the Long Island Collection of the East Hampton Library served as a repository of information regarding the U. S. Life Saving Service on Long Island. Gina Piastuck, director of the collection, was tremendously helpful with material from the Henry E. Huntting Collection, which contained documents and receipts pertaining to Huntting's years (1869-1885) as superintendent of Long Island stations within the system's Third District. Gina's kindness, patience, and encouragement were most appreciated. Thanks to her husband, Jason Piastuck, for his expertise in the preparation of several images used in this book.

Her two assistants, Steve Boerner and Andrea Meyer, were equally helpful in scanning a number of the Huntting documents, and providing images from both the East Hampton and Montauk libraries.

Special thanks to former Montauk Library archivist Robin Strong, who provided a number of shipwreck images. Her knowledge of Montauk is both invigorating and inspiring.

Boatswains Mate Senior Chief Petty Officer Eric Best of U. S. Coast Guard Station Montauk graciously permitted access to the station property for photographs and provided information on some of the officers in charge at the station over the years. He and Machinery Technician 2nd Class Brian Giunta were happy to cooperate and showed professional courtesy. They are a credit to the service. And thanks to former Coast Guard officer-in-charge at Station Montauk, Jason Walter (currently associated with the Montauk Point Lighthouse Museum) for his knowledge of Station Montauk and assistance in gaining access to the Station.

Timothy Dring, Commander, U.S. Naval Reserve (retired), provided images and histories of the Montauk Life Saving and Coast Guard stations. He proved to be very congenial and genuinely interested in this project.

Honorable mention goes to former Southold Historical Society Director Geoffrey Fleming and the Society's collections manager Amy Folk, for allowing access to a journal kept by the lifesavers at the Ditch Plain Station in the 1870s. Also, to John Cooney, representing the historical Quogue Life Saving Station, for permission to use images of Frank Warner.

Special thanks to Coast Guard Atlantic Area Historian, William H. Thiesen, for providing direction in acquiring data about Coast Guard Station Montauk.

Much appreciation goes to Isabel Carmichael of the East Hampton Historical Society for taking time out from her busy schedule to edit my work.

Lastly, I thank my wife, Terrianne, for her love and patience when I hibernated to do my work, and when I spent hours away from home accumulating material. She is my lifesaver.

A LEGACY OF VALOR

"The Life Line" by Winslow Homer (1836-1910), done in 1884, combines the drama of the shipwreck, the forces of nature, and the desperate struggle to survive.

ACKNOWLEDGEMENTS

*The Montauk Point Lighthouse is shown in 1871.
A boathouse for the Life Saving Service existed on the
property at that time.
(National Archives)*

Prologue

What do you think is the grandeur of storms and dismemberments and the deadliest battles and wrecks and the wildest fury of the elements and the power of the sea.... Master of the spasms of the sky and of the shatter of the sea, Master of nature and passion and death, And of all terror and pain. (Leaves of Grass, Walt Whitman, 1855)

WHEN LIFESAVING STATIONS first made their appearance on the rugged, remote, windswept peninsula of Montauk, there were only four other structures in existence: First House, Second House, Third House, and the Montauk Point Lighthouse. Built in 1796, the Lighthouse stood at the extreme eastern tip of Long Island. The other three dwellings, spaced about four miles apart, served as homes for shepherds and keepers of the thousands of cattle and sheep that grazed upon the hills of Montauk in the spring and summer months in a tradition that began in the 1660s and continued until the 1920s.

First House, originally built in 1744 and rebuilt in 1798, stood within the boundaries of the present Hither Hills State Park. Its keeper was responsible for entering the earmarks of the cattle and sheep on the common pasture list and assuring that fences were properly maintained. It burned down in 1909.

Second House, built in 1746 and rebuilt in 1797, is located on the main road at the west end of Montauk village. Its keeper tended the sheep to the west and the cattle to the east, making certain there were no crossovers.

Third House, originally built in 1747 and replaced in 1806, is situated within present-day Montauk County Park. The keeper here was responsible for the entire pasture and oversaw the annual roundup each year in spring when the herds would be paraded from East Hampton and Amagansett to Indian Field. Then, around November 1st, the animals were rounded up and paraded back to their farms for the winter.

The remoteness of Montauk and the lack of population in those early days made it difficult when a ship fell victim to storm, fog, or other form of maritime peril. The first lifesaving station in the area was established at Amagansett in 1849, some 10 miles distant from the present town of Montauk and 16 miles from the Montauk Point Lighthouse. About six years later two stations and a boathouse were established across the Montauk shores.

Charles Lanman (1819-1895), author, explorer, and government official, visited Montauk around 1870 and made note of some of the maritime calamities that occurred there:

Among the more noted vessels lost on Montauk Point were the schooner Triumph, the whale ship Forrester, the brig Marcellus, the bark Algea, the light boat Nantucket, the brig Flying Cloud, the ship John Milton, and the steamship Amsterdam, laden with fruit from Malaga.

◄ A LEGACY OF VALOR

The incidents which have been narrated to me touching these various calamities do not incline me to fall in love with the ocean on the score of humanity, and I was surprised to learn that much the larger proportion of the poor mariners wrecked on the coast of Montauk had been saved. The most fearful calamity was that which befell the ship John Milton, and her wreck was almost the first object that I saw and sketched on my first visit to the region, and it was long before I could banish the story of her fate from my mind.... Not content with having sent this noble ship upon the shore, the ocean for some weeks was unceasingly hammering away with its huge and savage breakers upon the timbers of the poor hulk, until every vestige had disappeared forever. And thus has it been in every clime; "man marks the earth with ruin; his control stops with the shore."

Ships encountered numerous mishaps as they entered the waters off Montauk for many years, until 20th-century improvements in technology improved response times for lifesavers to ships in distress. Such improvements resulted in a reduction in the number of lifesaving stations along the shores of Long Island. The following pages tell the story of the Montauk Life Saving and Coast Guard Stations, plus 107 maritime incidents in Montauk waters, and their place in the fabric of Long Island Life Saving and Coast Guard history.

PROLOGUE

*First House, ca. 1900.
Built in 1744 and rebuilt in 1798, this was the first dwelling
travelers would encounter as they approached Montauk.
(Peg Winski)*

*Second House, ca. 1900.
Built in 1746 and rebuilt in 1797, this is Montauk's oldest existing dwelling.
The Montauk Historical Society leased it from the Town of East Hampton
in 1968 to open a museum there. (Montauk Library)*

*Third House, 1900.
Built in 1747 and rebuilt in 1806, the keeper was responsible
for the entire pasture and oversaw the annual livestock roundup.
It is now part of Montauk County Park.
(Montauk Library)*

CHAPTER 1

General History of the U. S. Life Saving Service

The broken skeletons of wrecked vessels with which the beaches are strewn and with which the ever changing sands are busying themselves, here burying and there exhuming, the unmarked mounds with the graveyards of the scattered elements abound, sorrowfully testify to the vastness of the sacrifice of life and property which these inexorable shores have claimed. (Brooklyn Daily Eagle, March 18, 1877)

THE BEGINNINGS OF a lifesaving service in the United States began with the Humane Society of Massachusetts, which erected shelters and stationed boats along the coast of the state in 1789. The first lifeboat station was built at Cohasset in 1791.

With the growth of shipping after the American Revolution, Secretary of the Treasury Alexander Hamilton created the Revenue Marine on April 22, 1790. Its chief purpose was to enforce the Tariff Act of 1789, protect American goods, and stop the smuggling of foreign products into the country. However, lifesaving efforts were handled by groups of unorganized volunteers who basically did the best they could with what skills and equipment they had. "If anything unusual was sighted along shore — a ship in peril — the family horn was blown, which signal the next neighbor passed on … At the sound of the rally every man left his plow or trowel or shop or sermon … and made for the beach."[1]

In 1831 the Revenue Marine's cutters were ordered to "render assistance to vessels in distress and to save life and property at sea by patrolling areas near their stations during the winter."[2]

In 1848 William A. Newell (1817-1901), a New Jersey congressman, appealed to Congress for $10,000 to provide equipment to assist people who were victims of shipwrecks along the shores of the state. While living in Manahawkin, he was a volunteer for shipwrecks across Barnegat Bay. His frustration of observing a terrible wreck and loss of life, and realizing that volunteers were unable to save the doomed passengers, led to the idea of forming a lifesaving organization.

The resulting Newell Act of 1848 allowed for the establishment of stations between Sandy Hook and Little Egg Harbor along the New Jersey coast. In March 1849 the Life-Saving Benevolent Association of New York was established, which successfully lobbied Congress to create a total of twenty-four stations along the shores of New Jersey and Long Island, including one at Amagansett. The stations were to be administered by the U. S. Revenue Marine (later the U. S. Revenue Cutter Service) within the Treasury Department.

*Alexander Hamilton (1755-1804)
As Secretary of State in 1790 he created the Revenue Cutter
Service, a forerunner of the lifesaving service.*

It was a start, but since the stations were manned by volunteers and situated about 10 miles distant from each other, this meant long stretches of shoreline had to be patrolled. Though well intended and stocked with plenty of necessary equipment, they were poorly organized, resembling a volunteer fire department with no one in charge. To add to the disorganization, no inspections were conducted to insure that men and equipment were up to standards. Eaton's Neck on Long Island's North Shore was the site of the first station in 1849. By 1855 there were 15 stations operating on Long Island, including two at Montauk: Ditch Plain and Hither Plain, plus a boathouse on the grounds of the Montauk Point Lighthouse. Despite difficulties in operation, they still rescued many people. However, because of their being located in such isolated locations, it took much longer for additional aid to arrive as compared to stations located near established communities to the west.

Lighthouses played a role in the lifesaving efforts of the nation. In 1820 a total of 55 light stations were maintained by the federal government. Navigation was tricky at best in those days, with reliance primarily on often inaccurate and unreliable charts from foreign nations in order to safely navigate our own waters.

It wasn't until the Blunts made creditable surveys and published charts in their *American Coast Pilot* that America had a reliable source for navigation. Edmund March Blunt (1770-1862) published the first edition in 1796. After thirty years, his sons George William (1802-1878) and Edmund (1799-1866) continued the work, making improvements in the publication. A total of 21 editions were produced by the Blunts until

1867, when the rights were sold to the Coast Survey, which continues the publication today.

By 1837 there were 208 lighthouses in the United States, but their contributions to improving navigation were not given proper attention until the creation of the Light-House Board in 1852. By then the number of lighthouses had reached 320, only seven of which were outfitted with the efficient Fresnel lenses developed in France by Augustin Fresnel (1788-1827) in 1822.

By the Civil War there were nearly 500 active lighthouses in the country, all fitted with Fresnel lenses. During the war some 135 lighthouses within the borders of the Confederacy were extinguished, as it was felt their bright beams would aid Northern ships. Following the war these lights were restored and by 1876 there were 637 lighthouses and 30 lightships functioning in the nation. In addition, numerous beacons, buoys, and fog signals were established to mark harbors, channels, and rivers; however, shipwrecks and loss of life continued to plague the coastlines.

The East End of Long Island, specifically the Town of East Hampton, was, for its first 250 years, an out-of-the-way region. Home to farmers, whalers, and fishermen and frequented by a few "from away," its lonely, rocky, and remote shores were unforgiving to the many ships and boats that strayed off course.

Jacqueline Overton noted that lifesaving in the early days was a community effort, not restricted to the volunteers struggling along the stormy coastlines: "Housewives built fires, made coffee, and prepared stores of lint, blankets, and flannels. If the surf ran not too high the men rowed out to the ship and rescued the seamen who were often brought in half dead to be tenderly nursed and cared for."[3]

Although they were a very small, ill-equipped group of volunteers in those days, these men did make a difference. Wrote Overton, "You may judge how much aid they were able to give when on the Long Island coast alone during the winter of 1850 nearly three hundred lives were saved by the prompt and vigorous action of the hardy surf-men."[4]

The lifesaving system operated in this ragtag fashion until a severe storm struck the East Coast in 1854. As a result, many sailors died because there were an insufficient number of stations and properly cared-for equipment.

Congress responded by appropriating funds for additional stations and to employ a full-time paid keeper at each one. New stations narrowed the distance between each one to just four or five miles. In addition, money was provided to hire two superintendents to supervise the stations along the New Jersey and Long Island coasts. Although crews were still manned by volunteers, and problems still existed, the beginnings of structure were evident.

The Civil War delayed further government activity in the improvement of the lifesaving system. Then, following another horrific East Coast storm in 1870 that caused much destruction and many casualties, Congress responded by creating six-man crews for existing stations and made plans to create several more.

In 1871, Sumner Increase Kimball (1834-1923), a young Maine attorney, was appointed chief of the Treasury Department's Revenue Marine Division. He succeeded in gaining an appropriation of $200,000 and Congress authorized the Secretary of the Treasury to employ crews of surfmen wherever necessary and for as long as they were needed. Kimball instituted six-man boat crews at all stations, built new ones, drew up regulations with standards of performance for crew members, set station routines and physical standards; in other words, he made the service a respectable and professional organization.

In August 1871, Captain John Faunce (1806-1891) of the U.S. Marine Service completed an examination of the Long Island coast with a view to perfecting a system of providing aid to victims of shipwrecks. The examination began at Montauk Point and continued west along the South Shore toward New York. The East Hampton Town sites visited were described as follows: "Montauk Point; Ditch Plain, at an old house opposite Great Pond; Hither Plain; Napeague Beach; Amagansett; Georgica Pond."

Captain Faunce thought the station at Napeague Beach, located between Amagansett and Montauk, should be called Mosquito Station "on account of the number, size and ferocity of the gallinippera [mosquitoes] there." He noted "rare and curious insects of the excessively annoying kind can be found anywhere along the beaches in that neighborhood, in sizes and quantities large enough to satisfy the most ambitious entomologist."[5]

*Sumner Increase Kimball (1834-1923).
He was general superintendent of the U.S. Life-saving Service
during its entire existence from 1878 to 1915. The success and integrity
of the service is credited largely to his leadership.*

Faunce reported that the houses used by men and equipment appeared to be no more than shanties, not conducive to winter months. Keepers were paid $250 a year and "when a vessel was wrecked in a gale or at night she was saved (if possible) by volunteers who would go down to the beach in hope of being able to save somebody's life. It does not require a vivid imagination to appreciate the dangers those men have encountered through pure desire to benefit their fellow being in peril." When the houses weren't used, fishing or gunning parties used them, taking whatever equipment they needed. There were also concerns about acts of vandalism.

Faunce proposed the reorganization of the system, improving the quality of the structure, positioning stations three and a half miles apart, hiring "good surfmen, without regard to politics," improving salaries and paying monthly, maintaining one man in summers to guard and maintain property.[6]

Lifesaving stations went through a number of identification changes. The Montauk stations were assigned as follows:

	Montauk Point	Ditch Plain	Hither Plain
1860s	No. 26	No. 25	No. 24
1873	No. 1	No. 2	No. 3
1874	No. 3	No. 4	No. 5
1878	No. 6	No. 7	No. 8
1883	Montauk Point	Ditch Plain	Hither Plain

The stations were identified by name until the creation of the U. S. Coast Guard in 1915.

The number of stations soon increased. In 1874, the stations were expanded to include the Maine coast, and ten sites south of Cape Henry, Virginia, including the Outer Banks of North Carolina. In 1875 stations were built along the Delaware-Maryland-Virginia peninsula, the Great Lakes, and the Florida coast. Stations later appeared in the Gulf of Mexico, along the West Coast, as well as a station at Nome, Alaska.

In the annual report for 1876, an ominous description of the Long Island region made apparent the necessity of having the lifesaving service:

> ...the Long Island and New Jersey coasts present the most ghastly record of disaster. Lying on either side of the gate to the great metropolis of the nation [New York City], they annually levy a terrible tribute upon its passing commerce. The broken skeletons of wrecked vessels with which the beaches are strewn...sorrowfully testify to the vastness of the sacrifice of life and property which these inexorable shores have claimed.[7]

In 1878 the growing network of lifesaving stations was finally organized as a separate agency of the Treasury Department and named the United States Life-Saving Service. On March 11, 1878, New York State Representative James W. Covert, in a speech before the House of Representatives, spoke of the historical background and necessity for the lifesaving service, and cited Long Island as a prime example:

> "I speak from actual experience when I say that very many of the surf-men on the Long Island coast at least...are among the best men of the community. They are men of intelligence, owning their own homes, supporting families—thrifty, forehanded, and enterprising. During the seasons when not thus employed, they are engaged mainly in surf-fishing; and in this way they gain correct and intimate knowledge of every foot of ground upon which they work and of every phase and feature of the surf in which they labor. They do not depend upon the pittance received from the Government for their support; it comes to them simply as a small addition to their yearly income, earned at seasons when they cannot prosecute their usual work. These men would not consent to enlist in the Navy, subject at the call of the Government to leave their families at any juncture, for possibly a long absence from home. Their home interests are in many instances too large; their home ties too strong, to permit many of them as prudent men to do this. This class of people have in great measure made the lifesaving service what it is. They have established local reputations for bravery and devotion upon the occasion of many a sad scene of shipwreck and disaster....I hazard nothing in

> *saying that nowhere upon the battle-field, where royal effort has been made to outdo the brightest deeds of gallantry, have greater self-sacrifice and more supreme devotion to duty been shown, than have been displayed on many an occasion of shipwreck and disaster on the storm-tossed line of coast from Maine to Florida.*[8]

That year, *Appleton's Annual Cyclopedia and Register of Important Events of the Year 1878*, lauded the actions of the lifesavers on Long Island:

> *The record of the Long Island and New Jersey beaches is terrible. The traveler upon them sees everywhere, protruding from the sands, the skeletons of wrecks, and their old-time story is only of innumerable drowned crews. Here were the earliest and the greatest successes of the Life-saving Service, whose programme [sic] devoted this entire line of beach to complete life-saving stations.*[9]

Sumner Kimball was selected as the General Superintendent of the Service, a position he would retain for the entire existence of the organization. The law which created the U. S. Coast Guard in 1915 also provided for the retirement of Kimball. The Service's reputation for honest, efficient, and non-partisan administration, plus performance of duty, can be attributed largely to his efforts.

Kimball organized beach patrols that were maintained through the end of World War II. These patrols were to be made on foot. He brought to an end a system that was not only disorganized, but one that had selected keepers based on political affiliations and personal favors. In the early days of the service, before the institution of Civil Service regulations, those assigned to a particular station could be removed for political reasons regardless of the quality of their service to the organization. For example, in a letter dated December 17, 1877, surfman Abram Loper (1836-1919), assigned to the station at Ditch Plain, Montauk, in 1872, wrote that he (himself) was:

> *considered a good and efficient surfman... [and] was appointed an oarsman in the crew... by the Keeper Samuel Straton [sic] and he believes he was appointed solely upon his merits as a surfman; that in the year of 1874 this deponent was removed by the orders of Henry Huntting Superintendent together with the rest of the crew, and others substituted by said Huntting who were not efficient men; And this deponent further saith that...he was removed on account of his political standing.*[10]

Another surfman, Jonathan Payne* (1832-1906), in a letter dated December 11, 1877, also stated he was considered a good surfman, that he had been appointed to the Hither Plain Station in 1873, that he "always fulfilled the duties of a member of the crew and that there was no fault found with this deponent as to his efficiency." However, he too was removed from the service by Superintendent Henry E. Huntting in 1874 "because of his political opinions."[11]

The overall success of the lifesaving service on Long Island during Kimball's time can be measured by the fact that only one Long Island surfman lost his life over the entire course of the service's existence: Charles H. Church of the Mecox (Bridgehampton) station drowned while crossing a sea puss (undertow) while on patrol in December 1903.

Lifesaving stations were now manned by full-time crews during the period when wrecks were most likely to occur. On Long Island and the rest of the East Coast this was usually between November and April, and was thus known as the "active season." In 1871 crews had been on duty at each alternate station only during winter months. By 1898 all stations were manned ten months out of the year, and by the early 1900s were covered year round.

During the summer of 1900 the Long Island stations became the reformed Fourth District of the Life Saving Service.

The greatest days of the Life Saving Service were during the years 1871 to 1881, when some of its greatest rescues were performed. Auxiliary organizations were established during this period to provide assistance as needed. The purpose of the Blue Anchor Society, formed in 1880, is described in the *Annual Report of the Life-Saving Service for the Fiscal Year Ended June 30, 1913*:

> ...to furnish relief to sick, injured, and destitute survivors of marine casualties and other situations of distress or misfortune. This benevolent society has been of invaluable assistance in the humanitarian work of alleviating pain, suffering, and want among the unfortunates temporarily in the care of the life-saving crews. The headquarters of the association is located in New York City, from which point, upon application, stores, consisting of boxes of clothing, blankets, restoratives, etc., are forwarded direct to the stations, without expense to the Government.[12]

The Women's National Relief Association was founded in 1881. Among its duties was to supply lifesaving stations with beds, blankets, warm clothing, and other necessities for victims of shipwrecks. Its first president was Lucretia Rudolph Garfield (1832-1918), the wife of President James Garfield.

Sumner Kimball realized the significance of public opinion regarding the lifesaving service, since all developments resulted from public pressure. To that end he made sure that the service was represented at a number of public events including the Philadelphia Centennial Exposition in 1876, and the Lewis and Clark Centennial Exposition held in Portland, Oregon, in 1905. At such events a complete station, with crew and equipment, was on display and demonstrations performed.

Kimball made certain the existence of the Life Saving Service reached the public in written form as well. The *Annual Reports*, which were published each year during the entire existence of the Service (1876-1914), serve to illustrate some of the most interesting stories of wreck and rescue in print, while giving the overall impression of the usefulness and necessity of the Service itself.

As the 20th century approached, two problems faced the Service. First, with the advent of steam-powered ships, the age of sail was coming to an end. Ships were now less at the mercy of the wind and in less danger of being driven ashore. Second, there was a notable increase of small, gasoline-powered boats, especially for recreational purposes. This led to a noticeable increase of incidents involving this type of vessel from 1905 to 1914; something the Service was ill equipped to handle.

*Lucretia Rudolph-Garfield (1832-1918)
Wife of President James Garfield, she was the
founder and first president of the Women's National Relief
Association in 1881, which supplied lifesaving stations with
necessities for shipwreck victims.*

There were other problems as well. There was no retirement system or any compensation for injured crewmen, and salaries became too low to attract new men. As a result, by 1914 men in their 60s and 70s were still on active duty, and, after years of trying to obtain a retirement system, Kimball agreed that a merger of the U. S. Revenue Cutter System and the U. S. Life-Saving Service would be best for all concerned. The merger was a wise decision, especially since the Progressive Movement was actively looking to eliminate excessive government spending during the 1910s. After careful examination, it was determined that the

Revenue Cutter Service proved to be the most wasteful.

An executive order from President Woodrow Wilson created the United States Coast Guard on January 28, 1915, which combined the two aforementioned services and provided for the retirement of Kimball and many of the older keepers and surfmen. Lifesaving keepers became warrant officers and surfmen became enlisted men, but few changes were made in the daily operations of the system.[13]

Under the new organization, the stations at Montauk became part of the Fourth District, the same number as for the Life Saving Service.

The Life Saving Service performed nobly during its existence. Though lasting only 37 years, the Service made an impact on American maritime history by the saving of a significant number of people by a group of brave and selfless men.

The organization that Sumner Kimball formed provided the basis for the new Coast Guard's search and rescue operation for years to come. One can find little fault with the thoroughness of his organization. The constant attention to practice with rescue equipment and inspections continues to this day. Basically, the good practices of the old Life Saving Service still prevail.

Dennis R. Means summed it up well:

> *From the beginning, its primary goal had been to save lives and property from the ravages of sea and storm. Between 1871 and 1915, when the Life Saving Service rejoined the Revenue Cutter Service to form the U. S. Coast Guard, the service assisted 28,121 disasters and shipwrecks and preserved the lives of 174,682 persons and $288,871,237 worth of vessels and cargo. Although mere cold statistics to warm and complacent Americans today, such figures are indicative of a legacy of valor and skill the likes of which this country may never see again.[14]*

Joseph Francis (1801-1893)
Inventor of the Francis metallic style surfboat, he was awarded
a gold medal from Congress in 1890 for his lifesaving invention.

*Francis surfboat.
Invented by Joseph Francis in 1845, it was placed in service
five years later and saved thousands of lives over the years.
(U.S. Coast Guard)*

Equipment, Procedures, and Personnel

Most stations were in isolated areas and crewmen were required to launch their boats from the beach into the surf. The Life Saving Service had two means of rescuing people from ships stranded near shore: by boat and by a strong line stretched from the beach to the vessel. The Service boats were either a 700 to 1,000-pound, self-bailing, self-righting surfboat pulled by six surfmen with 12 to 18-foot oars, or a 2 to 4–ton lifeboat. The surfboat could be pulled on a cart by crewmen, or horses, to a site near the wreck and then launched into the surf. The lifeboat could be fitted with sails for work farther offshore and was used in very heavy weather.

Among the various designs of surfboats, several of them were used at the Montauk stations.

The Raymond surfboat was built by William Raymond in 1807 and resembled the whaleboats of the late 1700s. It was lined with cork to provide extra flotation. Thirty feet in length and manning a crew of 12, the vessel could accommodate 20 people and performed admirably under stormy conditions.

The first corrugated metallic life surfboat was invented by Joseph Francis (1801-1893) in 1845 and placed in service by 1850. Made of iron and easy to lift by surfmen, it could hold four passengers and was a successful alternative to heavy wooden boats that could easily be damaged on rocks. Thanks to his invention, thousands of lives were saved, and in 1890, Congress issued Francis a gold medal for his efforts.

Frederick C. Beebe (1839-1923), a private boat builder from Greenport, Long Island, designed the Beebe pulling surfboat. Neither self-righting nor self-bailing, it was about 27 feet in length and 7 feet wide with a cedar-planked hull over white oak frames.

Beebe and Lt. Charles H. McLellan, assistant inspector of the Third District of the Life Saving Service in the 1870s, developed the beach-launched surfboat bearing their names. Self-bailing and self-righting, it was 25 feet in length and 7 feet in width. Its hull was made of white cedar planks over white oak frames with galvanized iron fasteners. This model virtually replaced all previous designs and was generally in use from 1888. The bulk of these craft were built at the Beebe Boatyard in Greenport from 1887 to 1918.

The Race Point surfboat was designed at Race Point, at the tip of Cape Cod, Massachusetts. Neither self-righting nor self-bailing, it was 24.5 feet in length, 6 feet wide, and constructed of cypress or cedar planks over oak frames, with copper or galvanized iron fasteners.

GENERAL HISTORY OF THE U. S. LIFE SAVING SERVICE

*Beebe-McLellan surfboat
Developed by Frederick Beebe and Lt. Charles H. McClellan, it
became the standard craft in the Life Saving Service in the 1880s.
(U.S. Coast Guard)*

*Self-righting Life Boat in action ca. 1879
(U.S. Coast Guard)*

The Monomoy surfboat originated at Monomoy Island off Cape Cod, and was 26 feet in length and nearly 7 feet in width. It was similar to the Race Point model, being neither self-righting nor self-bailing and having cedar planking over oak frames and galvanized fasteners.

When a ship wrecked close to shore and the seas were too rough to launch a boat, a mortar was used to fire a strong hawser (line) out to the stranded vessel. A 24-pound ball could be launched about 1,200 feet.

To aid in signaling ships from shore (and from ship to ship), the Coston signal flare was introduced in 1859. Developed by Martha Coston (1826-1904) in 1858, it was used to warn ships that strayed too close to shore and to let wrecked vessels know that they were spotted and that help would be forthcoming. The device was so effective that it was used into the 1930s. All boats continue to be required to carry similar flares in the event of distress.

In 1877 the cannon-like Lyle gun was introduced. Developed by David A. Lyle (1845-1937), it consisted of a gun weighing 163 pounds, which fired an 18-pound metal projectile. Lighter and easier to use than the old mortars, the gun could shoot a projectile up to 1,800 feet. It carried a small messenger line by which the shipwrecked sailors were able to pull out the heavier hawser. Another advantage of the gun was its bronze construction, helping it to resist corrosion in salt water.

Once the line was shot to the ship, crew members aboard would tie it off to a mast or something equally sturdy. Then the life car could be pulled back and forth between the wreck and the shore. The life car resembled a small submarine and could be hauled over, through, or even under the sea. After the hatch was sealed, there was enough air inside to accommodate 11 people for three minutes. Typically, a life car carried 4 to 6 people, but since they weighed 250 pounds they were heavy and difficult to handle. In addition, the cramped quarters caused more than a few cases of panic in its passengers. It was soon replaced by the breeches buoy, which resembled a cork life preserver ring with canvas pants attached. It could be pulled out to the ship by pulleys enabling the endangered sailor to step into the ring and pants and then be pulled safely to shore. An individual climbed into it the same way as putting on a pair of pants.

The Lyle gun proved to be so effective that it was used until 1952 when it was replaced with the use of rockets.

Firing the Lifeline.

The Lyle Gun was introduced in 1877 by David A. Lyle and provided a lifeline to those in distress. The line is shown here being fired as part of a drill.
(Montauk Point Lighthouse Museum)

GENERAL HISTORY OF THE U. S. LIFE SAVING SERVICE

The breeches buoy is shown in two images. During its existence,
hundreds of lives were saved along Long Island's shores.
(Montauk Point Lighthouse Museum)

The iceboat, which was effective on both water and ice, was first developed by the Bellport Station, Long Island, enabling crews to reach the station in winter months.

The men who made up the crews of the Service were known as surfmen, because those on the East Coast launched their boats from open beaches into the surf. Most listed their occupations before entering the Service as "fisherman" or "mariner."

Superintendents in each district selected the keepers, the position of which "will be recognized at once as one of the most important in the Service," wrote Sumner Kimball. He added, "The indispensable qualifications for appointment are that he shall be of good character and habits, not less than 21 nor more than 45 years of age; have sufficient education to be able to transact the station business; be able-bodied, physically sound, and a master of boat craft and surfing."[15] Kimball made it clear that the keeper was indeed in charge and had the final say with whatever transpired at his station. Keepers (actually referred to as "captains") did the station paperwork and filed reports as necessary.

The *Brooklyn Daily Eagle* described the keeper's role in 1888:

> *The keeper is the animating soul of the station. It is to him the crew looks for inspiration and guidance. The discipline which makes these seven men as one in fidelity to duty emanates from him. The vigilance of the lonely night patrol upon the Winter beach, which lets no vessel strand unobserved and is to the service like an unsleeping eye, depends upon his own vigilance. In the hour of peril to the wrecked vessel it is his spirit that determines whether the men he commands shall prove heroes or cowards, whether the rescue shall succeed or fail, whether life shall be saved or lost and honor or shame befall the service and the nation.*[16]

In 1889, the Service consisted of 227 stations, 39 of which were on Long Island. That year the Service became uniformed, but, instead of resulting in an esprit de corps, it caused outrage since the surfmen were expected to pay for the uniforms out of their meager salaries.

Each day of the week, except Sunday, the surfmen were expected to drill or clean. On Mondays and Thursdays the crew practiced with the beach apparatus, rigging the equipment, and firing the Lyle gun. On Tuesdays, they practiced with their boats, which included intentionally capsizing and righting the boats as part of a simulated emergency. The rest of the week was devoted to signal practice and first aid. Saturdays were spent cleaning the station.

There was one other important duty that constituted a significant portion of the surfman's routine: lookout and patrol duties. During daylight hours, a surfman was assigned to scan the nearby water area from the lookout tower.

Surfmen conducted beach patrols at night or in poor weather. At first, distances were set up so that each patrol would meet others from a neighboring station. As more and more of the coast came under the watchful eye of the Service, this sort of coverage became impossible to maintain. In areas where overlapping patrols could not be maintained, the surfmen patrolled for five miles or more.

In the early years of the Life Saving Service, surfmen only worked during winter months and conducted walking patrols about two and a half miles in each direction between stations. If a ship was observed to be in distress a flare was sent up to alert the other surfmen. If the situation was severe, flares were sent up to alert neighboring stations to assist.

Launching a small boat into rough seas was the most important part of the job, something for which lifesavers were intensely trained. Usually the crew waited until there was a lull ("slatch") between waves.

Then, on signal, the cry of "Shove 'r in!" was heard and they rushed into the restless waves.

According to former East Hampton historian Jeannette Edwards Rattray, once in the water, eyes focused on the captain. "The men at the oars must have implicit confidence in the captain. He stands in the stern facing the breakers, and steers. They must never look over their shoulders, just watch his face and follow his orders."[17]

Wrecks generally occurred at night and during winter months when conditions were suitably rough. Consequently, lifesavers performed their duties under very difficult circumstances. It was not unusual, during severe weather, to see a man returning from his patrol soaked to the skin and half frozen. An account of a surfman on Fire Island serves to illustrate:

> ... a patrolman named Allen had to keep behind the dunes, only to surmount them long enough to attempt to observe the fury of wind and sea. When Allen finally arrived at the shack [a halfway house between stations] much later than usual, he found that the lantern, although extinguished, was still a little warm. He surmised that the [beach patrol] man he was to have met, had waited and finally left. Exhausted and warmed by the fire, Allen fell asleep, but awakened to what he thought was a cannon shot. Hearing nothing further, he decided to return to his station. He donned his oilskins, backed out into the furious storm, and latched the door shut behind.

Sending up a Coston signal flare. These signals proved effective in alerting ships that came too close to shore.
(Montauk Point Lighthouse Museum)

He paused just long enough to look toward the sky for any sign of a break in the storm. Allen was flabbergasted. Directly above him and jutting over the shack, was the bowsprit of an enormous, three-masted schooner!

A man, still alive, his arms and legs frozen to the bowsprit, stared down at him. Allen rescued him, then clambered onto the ship, which was already breaking up, leaving no time to go for assistance. One by one, he chopped seven more crewmen out of the ice and carried them to safety.

At daylight, Allen's captain and two surfmen...met him and the sailors whose lives he had saved. With typical Life Saving Station modesty, the unemotional captain made the following brief entry into his logbook:

'Three-masted schooner Beaumont came ashore in heavy gale two miles west of station and crew of eight were assisted ashore by surfman Allen.'[18]

As the lifesaving station crew's motto states, "You have to go out, but you don't have to come back." Through the eyes of James Howard Hand (1871-1962), who was stationed at the Georgica Life Saving Station in East Hampton, we get an idea of how the surfmen spent their time when they weren't involved in rescue efforts:

A Lifeboat heading out to a ship in distress.
The motto of the lifesavers was "You have to go out,
but you don't have to come back."
(Montauk Point Lighthouse Museum)

Captain Nat Dominy Jr. was a good keeper. He would order a side of beef, or whatever else we needed, in large quantities. We all took turns in the cooking. Every third day we baked bread. We all learned to be good housekeepers. We took life fairly easy, in between wrecks. We had music. Will Gardner used to come up with his violin; Condit Miller played one too; Everett Hand made himself a banjo and played it by ear; we all sang.[19]

The men also hunted duck, geese, even whales. "We kept whaling gear on hand," said Charles Raynor Bennett (1862-1942) at Georgica station. "We could do most anything within hailing distance of the station. But one man always had to stay on watch."[20]

Besides the keeper and his six surfmen on duty there was the "seventh man." While the keeper was at the station year round, the crew of six was required to be on duty during those months considered most susceptible to wrecks. The "seventh man," added in 1895, would cover in cases of illness or leave. His tour of duty was shorter than the others.

A Lifesaver on Patrol.
(U.S. Coast Guard)

In the early years of the lifesaving service the Montauk station had six surfmen from September 1 to November 30 of each year, with the "seventh man" added from December 1 to April 30. Beginning in 1894 the six crewmen were on duty from August 22 to May 31 with the "seventh man" added between December 1 and April 30. By 1912 the tour of duty for the six surfmen was from August 1 to May 31, with the additional surfman from October 1 to May 31. This system lasted until May 1916.

Supplies of coal were necessary for all stations. An idea of how much was needed is noted in a notice posted at the East Hampton Post Office for bids to furnish fuel for the town stations: Ditch Plain, Napeague, and Georgica needed 12 tons each, while Hither Plain and Amagansett each required 10 tons.

In 1902 each of the lifesaving stations received a powerful megaphone for use in stormy weather. Another new piece of equipment, the Preparatory Long Distance signal, was added to the stations in October 1905. This consisted of a large black ball that was hoisted to the top of a signal pole whenever the station wished to signal a government cutter to pass nearer to them for communication purposes.

On Long Island, the first headquarters for the Life Saving Service was at Bridgehampton, headed by Superintendent Henry E. Huntting (1828-1903), also of Bridgehampton. He was originally trained as a cooper (repairer of barrels and casks) and used his skills at sea. He and his brother James (1825-1882) became mates aboard the *Jefferson*, and before long he commanded his own ship, the *Charles Carroll*. He was in command of the ship *Pacific* in 1863, when it was badly damaged and he was forced to return to Sag Harbor. During his retirement years, on 19 April 1869 he was appointed superintendent for the Third District of the Life Saving Service, serving until 1885. He later served in the New York State Legislature.

In 1873, the keepers of the stations in the Town of East Hampton were each earning $200 annually.[21] In 1876 the rate was still $200, with surfmen receiving $40 per month during active months when they were required to live at their assigned stations. At other times, their assistance with a shipwreck earned them an additional $3 each. By 1885 they were receiving $700 per annum.[22] Interestingly enough, in 1870 Representative Henry A. Reeves (1832-1916) proposed decreasing the keeper's $200-per-year pay to $50:

> *...because their duties are nominal rather than real; and when real services are rendered I would reward them ... At present this sum of $200 yearly paid to keepers...is in most cases a mere gratuity for which no actual or considerable service is performed. All they do from one year's end to another is to keep the key of the houses, occasionally enter them to see if the public property is undisturbed, and with periodical punctuality draw their quarterly pay. At many of the stations, the...apparatus are not taken from the houses for months, or it may be years at a time, and at every one of the stations the mere supervision and care of the property intrusted [sic] to the keeper would be abundantly compensated by the payment of fifty dollars a year...*
>
> *For years these places have been sought for and have been given out, not on the grounds of personal fitness or actual qualification of the applicant, but as rewards for partisan services... in many cases...[these keepers] were unable to render any service whatever...for the simple reason that they knew not how to handle a boat or the use the other apparatus of the station.*

HENRY E. HUNTTING, OF BRIDGEHAMPTON.

Henry E. Huntting (1828-1903) was first Superintendent of Third District Life Saving Stations, which included Long Island, from 1869 to 1885. His service was marred by complaints from surfmen removed from stations due to their political affiliations.

Reeves also proposed testing new equipment and if proven effective, to replace existing material. He concluded,

If there be other [areas]...whereon these stations might be advantageously located and efficiently maintained, I would lose no time in establishing them at such points. One human life is worth all the cost of lining our shores with these means for its rescue from the perils of shipwrecks.

Regardless of the pay rate, the role played by the station keeper was invaluable.
In the spring of 1880 a bill came before Congress to pension widows and orphans of lifesaving crews lost

in the line of service. The *Brooklyn Daily Eagle* considered it a "wise, humane and imperative measure."[23]

It was announced in December 1888 that the installation of telephones to all lifesaving stations on Long Island would begin in March 1889.

Arthur Dominy (1841-1918) served as Superintendent of Long Island Life Saving Stations from 1885 to 1915. He and Henry E. Huntting were the only two superintendents for the Long Island region for the entire existence of the Service.

When crews returned to duty in the Third District on September 1, 1893, 212 of 222 crewmen returned from the year before. This was not surprising, since the pay rate had been increased from $50 to $65 a month.

A law in 1894 declared that crews were to go on duty on August 1 instead of September 1 and remain until June 1 instead of May 1.

Arthur Dominy (1841-1918) of Bay Shore, Long Island, was appointed superintendent of Long Island Life Saving Stations in July 1885. He remained at his post until the service became part of the newly created United States Coast Guard in 1915. Dominy is credited with being instrumental in legislation passed to create pensions for those serving 25 years in the Service.

An interesting East Hampton rescue took place on July 7, 1883. A young man known only as Irvine was operating a catboat in Gardiner's Bay when he noticed a storm approaching. He began to haul ashore with his passenger, a 7-year-old girl named Anna Miller (1877-1924), of Amagansett. Suddenly the wind shifted and a sharp gust caused a jib in the boom, causing it to swing around and knock the girl overboard. Irvine dived in and grabbed her, but the rough waters caused them both to be in peril!

Witnessing the events from shore, 10-year-old Maria Dayton Parsons (1873-1893) launched a skiff, rowed almost a quarter-mile to the struggling pair, and in the impending storm managed to rescue both.

On February 7, 1888, after numerous accounts of Maria Parsons's efforts were given by witnesses, the Life Saving Service awarded her a silver medal that included this citation:

With great presence of mind and bravery she rescued the man and child from drowning. It was fortunate that Maria Parsons was skilled in the use of oars, otherwise her noble efforts would have proved fruitless, the courage and self possession she displayed considering her years deserves the highest commendation.

Long Island historian Noel Gish was not surprised. He noted in 1998, "How could young Maria not have been a good oarswoman? She was a Parsons, a member of one of East Hampton's oldest families. She grew up around the bays and oceans, the land and sea were one to her."[24]

The skeletal remains of a Montauk shipwreck (ca. 1930) serve
as a reminder of the dangers along its rocky coast.
(Montauk Library)

CHAPTER 2

Montauk Point Life Saving Station

THE PROPERTY OF the Montauk Point Lighthouse was the site of a lifeboat station. A ten-year lease was obtained for this purpose on February 17, 1853. By November of that year the Life Saving Benevolent Association noted that the lifeboat at the site had suffered significant damage since there was no structure to house it. A lifeboat house, 17 X 36 feet in size, was eventually constructed by 1855. It contained a shingle roof and cedar board siding.

Originally maintained by volunteers, paid surfmen took over in 1871, with its keeper being the "Light house keeper."

In early 1872, Lighthouse keeper Thomas Ripley (1821-1888) was listed as being in charge of the site, which was described as follows:

> *House 30 by 16, by 14 feet posts; in fair order; roof and door-sills require repairs.*
> *Recommendations – That house be painted two coats, estimated cost $65*
> *House be repaired, estimated cost $50*
> *Total $115*[25]

Also in 1872, the station was reclassified as Station No. 1 and in 1878 as Station No. 6.

Although there was never a permanent crew assigned to this station, the rescue boathouse existed at a location southwest of the Montauk Point Lighthouse at Turtle Cove and was known to be maintained by the crew of the Ditch Plain station by 1885. A Francis metallic pulling surfboat was maintained there from 1856, replaced by a Raymond-type surfboat in 1883.[26] For many years the site was listed as being "at the Light."

On December 13, 1872, Superintendent Huntting wrote a letter noting that there was "no accommodation for a crew" at Montauk Point and that "there is no man to take charge of the Station nearer than Amagansett, a distance of 14 miles. The Keeper would have to board (with consent of the Dept.) with the Light Keeper." Huntting added, "As this is a crew in No. 2 — a distance of 3½ miles from No. 1, there could keep a watch east and with the assistance of the Light Keeper and his Assistants could thoroughly cover the grounds of [the station]."

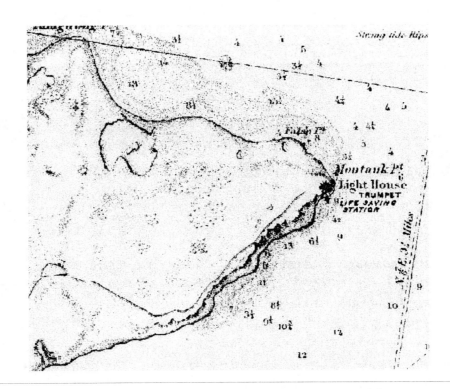

Chart showing location of the Montauk Point "Life Saving Station."
The equipment was maintained by neighboring
Ditch Plain Station.
(National Oceanic and Atmospheric Administration's
Office of Coast Survey)

Huntting went on to say that if a keeper should be assigned to the Station at Montauk Point, he "would respectfully recommend Elijah M. Bennett of Amagansett."[27] Nothing was done in this regard, and the boathouse remained in charge of the Lighthouse keeper.

The necessity of this station was noted in an 1895 news article, stating the station "has never been manned, a somewhat remarkable fact as the coast at the Point is one of the most dangerous on the Long Island shore and hardly a winter passes without a number of vessels going on the rocks at the foot of the Montauk cliffs."[28]

The first keeper noted was Jonathan A. Miller, who also served as keeper of Montauk Point Lighthouse 1865-1869 and 1872-1875. He received no salary because part of the lighthouse keeper's duties included overseeing the boathouse. Miller, born in Springs in 1834, had a hand blown off during a Civil War naval battle aboard the ship *Oneida*. He died October 29, 1915.

The boathouse at Montauk Point remained in existence until the commencement of the U.S. Coast Guard in 1915 at which time the facility was discontinued and the building removed.

Jonathan Miller (1834-1915) was believed to be the first keeper of the lifeboat station at Montauk, although he was actually keeper of the Montauk Point Lighthouse during the years 1865-1869 and 1872-1875.
(Montauk Point Lighthouse Museum)

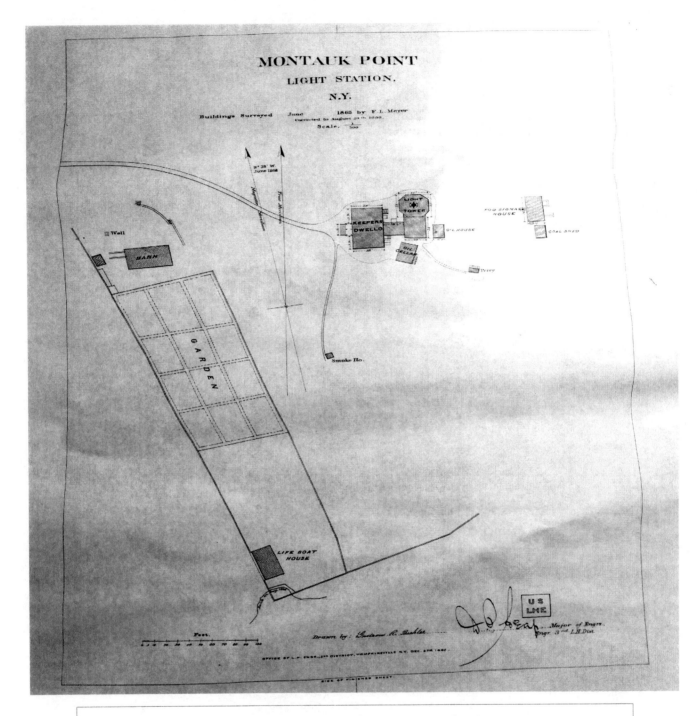

*Map of Montauk Point Light Station 1890 showing lifeboat house at bottom.
(Lighthouse Engineer, Third District, Lighthouse Service)*

The Montauk Point Lighthouse Station as it appeared in 1903. Among its numerous outbuildings was the lifeboat station, the roof of which is shown at lower right. By 1910 the lifeboat station was no longer listed as active. (Suffolk County Historical Society)

The boathouse overlooking Turtle Cove is shown from the top of Montauk Point Lighthouse ca. 1900. (Paul Driscoll collection, Montauk Point Lighthouse Museum)

The Montauk Point Lighthouse is shown prior to 1910. Note the lifesaving boat at lower right at the location of the lifesaving boathouse, which was maintained by the crew at the Ditch Plain Station.
(Montauk Point Lighthouse Museum)

CHAPTER 3

Ditch Plain Life Saving Station

LAND WAS CONVEYED for the station in 1854 and a boathouse, like the one at Montauk Point, was erected the following year. A Francis lifeboat was at the location.

In 1872, Samuel Stratton was listed as keeper, earning $200 annually. The "red house" design station building was described as being:

> 30 by 16, by 14 feet posts; in fair order; slight repairs necessary to roof and doors. An extra life-car (old pattern) at station.
> Recommendations—That an addition of 12 feet be built to the main house, estimated cost $450.
> House be ceiled [sic] throughout, estimated cost $169
> House be painted two coats, estimated cost $65
> House be repaired, estimated cost $50
> Total $734[29]

The building incorporated living quarters and boat storage under one roof.

In June 1886 the Secretary of the Treasury, Daniel Manning (1831-1887), ordered a new and larger station to be built at a cost of $4,000. The structure, L-shaped in design, contained living quarters on the main and second floors with a watch tower above.

Ditch Plain Life Saving Station shown in 1885. It was destroyed by a lightning strike in March 1891 and rebuilt. (Montauk Point Lighthouse Museum)

31

A LEGACY OF VALOR

In February 1888 the building came close to destruction when some crew members were making rubber cement (which contained benzene). In the process a lantern came into contact with the mixture, creating an explosion. Crew member Charles Miller's eyebrows were singed as a result, but he quickly threw the can of burning fluid outside to prevent the building from catching fire.

Though Miller's quick thinking did indeed prevent a catastrophe, there was nothing any of the crew could do when, during a freak winter thunderstorm on the night of Saturday, February 28, 1891, lightning struck and destroyed both the new building and the old 1855 structure.

Once the old building was struck, it quickly burned to the ground. Since the newer (1886) building was only about twenty-five feet to the east and the wind was driving the flames in that direction, Captain Frank Stratton quickly ordered the removal of as much property and equipment as could be saved from the new building.

There were no injuries but several members suffered losses in personal property, including many carpenter's tools. Captain Stratton, whose home was located nearby, opened his doors to the crew, and it was from his dwelling that lifesaving operations continued until a new building was erected.

In September 1891 a contract was awarded by the government to construct a new station, which "will be unlike anything on the coast, a departure from all previous plans in this line. The new station will be a large and handsome building."[30] The cost was to be $5,600. Construction was completed in 1892.

Ditch Plain Station was within the First Fuel District of the Life Saving Service. In 1895 the station required 12 tons of coal as part of its operation.

Originally described as being "three and one-half miles southward of Montauk Light," it was later changed by adding "abreast of Great Pond [Lake Montauk]."

Camp Wikoff was situated near the station in 1898. Consequently, the station saw much activity that summer, with newspaper headquarters, telegraph offices and the camp of the Signal Corps being located nearby.

A record of boats in 1902 showed the following craft at the station:

Model	Builder	Built	Placed at Station
Life-Francis	Joseph Francis, New York	1856	1856
Surf-Beebe	Frederick Beebe, Greenport	1882	1882
Raymond	L. Raymond, New York	1856	1883
Surf (open) Beebe	Frederick Beebe, Greenport	1892	1892[31]

Ditch Plain Life Saving Station

U.S. LIFE-SAVING SERVICE, Form 9.

INVENTORY OF PUBLIC PROPERTY at Station No. 4, District No. 2.

Articles	Quantities	Condition	Articles	Quantities	Condition	Articles	Quantities	Condition
Anchor			Hatchets			Powder, pounds of	10	
Anchor, boat			Hauling line, 2½-inch	1		Powder magazine		
Anchor, sand	1		Hauling line, 3-inch			Paint, Crockett's		
Augers			Hawsers, 3½-inch	1		Paint brushes	7	
Axes	2		Hawsers, 4-inch			Palms, sailors'	1	
Bags, for coal			Hawsers, 4½-inch			Paper		
Blankets	20		Haversacks, rubber			Pens, steel	24	
Blocks, double, 12-inch	2		Inkstand	1		Penholders	8	
Blocks, double and single, 8-inch	2		Ink			Pans, dish	3	
Blocks, assorted			Jack-plane	1		Pans, tin	1	
Boat, metallic	1		Journal	1		Plates, tin	24	
Boat, cedar	1		Kettle, tea	1		Pillows	10	
Boat carriage	1		Knives	12		Pliers	1	
Boat hooks, double			Knife, carving	1		Port-fires		
Boat hooks, double and warp	2		Ladders, 24-feet	1		Port-fire staff	1	
Boat grapnel	2		Lanterns, signal			Pole	1	
Boat hatchet	2		Lanterns, globe	3		Putty	2 lb	
Boat drag	1		Lanterns, dark, of brass	1		Patent dryer	2 lb	
Books, blank			Lamp wick	4 balls		Quick matches		
Books, receipt and expenditure	1		Lamp feeder	2		Rockets, line		
Buckets, rubber	2		Life car	2	1 no left	Rockets, signal	7	
Buckets, water	4		Life raft			Rocket wire	24	
Brooms, corn	2		Life preservers			Rocket range	1	
Brads, 1½-inch	4 lb		Line boxes	2		Rubber cloth		
Bull's eye and strap	1		Lead, red	1 keg		Reel for shot-line	1	
Calking irons, boat	1		Lead, white	1 can		Spun yarn	4 coil	
Camp stools	10		Manila, 9-thread	1 coil		Stove and fixtures	1	
Cans, iron, mess			Manila, 12-thread			Shovels	2	
Cans, tin, mess			Magazine, copper			Signal lights	6	
Chisels			Marline			Shot	24	
Chests	1		Marline-spike	2		Shot wire	14	
Clothes hooks			Marine glasses	1		Shot hooks	1	
Coal hod and shovel	1		Match safe			Shot lines, 500 yards	2	
Cots	10		Match staves			Speaking trumpet	1	
Comforters	10		Match rope			Sponges		
Crotch	1		Match range			Sand paper	6 sheets	
Coffee pot	1		Medicine chest			Signal flags		
Coffee can			Monkey-wrench	1		Skids	2	
Cups, tin	12		Mortar and bed	1		Spoons, iron, large	12	
Falls, manila, 2½-inch	1		Manila, 3-inch			Spoons, iron, small	12	
Falls, manila, 2¼-inch	1		Manila, 2½-inch			Sauce pan, 1-gallon	1	
Forks	12		Manila, 2¼			Straps, galvanized iron	2	
Forks, carving	1		Manila, 2-inch			Tacks, galvanized iron		
Files, hand-saw			Nails, galvanized			Tackles	2	
Gimlet	1		Nails, assorted	2 lb		Turpentine, quarts of	1 pint	
Grindstone, 14 by 16, wood box	1		Nails, boat	1½ lb		Tin can, for quick matches		
Gridiron	1		Nippers			Twine, hemp	2 balls	
Hand cart			Needles, sail	6		Water pail, galvanized	1	
Hand grapnel and warp			Oars, assorted	20		White lead		
Hand mallet	1		Oakum	2 lb		Wrench, boat carriage	1	
Hand-saw	1		Oil, lamp			Wood		
Halliards, signal			Oil, linseed			Zinc	2 pieces	
Hammers, claw	1		Oil, signal					

Received from _____ the foregoing articles and outfits, this ____ day of _____, 187_.

Samuel T Stratton, Keeper.

Inventory of Public Property for Station No. 2 (Ditch Plain), signed by keeper Samuel Stratton, March 31, 1873 (Henry Huntting Collection — Long Island Collection, East Hampton Library)

The crew assisted when, on April 12, 1906, fire was discovered within the grounds of the nearby Montauk Association, threatening the destruction of the cottages. Surfmen with fire buckets raced to the scene and extinguished the flames.

When the U.S. Coast Guard was created in 1915, the station became Station No. 65 in the service.

With the potential for America's involvement in World War I, a watch tower was erected at the station in the summer of 1917 and by September personnel were armed with navy rifles and revolvers while on patrol.

Through funds provided by the Public Works Administration, plans were announced in October 1933 for the construction of a new two-story frame station building. The installation of radio transmitting equipment took place in May 1934. Although listed as inactive in 1934 the station was back on the active list the following year and remained so through World War II.

Following the disastrous 1938 Hurricane on September 21, which caused incredible destruction on the shores of eastern Long Island, the station's boathouse was lost and the main building, which was being used for storage of equipment, sustained significant damage. The Race Point type pulling surfboat was damaged beyond repair. The Coast Guard called for the construction of hurricane-proof buildings at certain stations and repairs at others. An estimated $20,000 was required for new construction at Ditch Plain. A new Roosevelt Design building was constructed in 1938. Rectangular in shape with symmetrical wings, the first floor contained the mess hall, kitchen, office, bathroom, and two bedrooms. The second floor had four small bedrooms and a bathroom. The attic was used for storage and was topped by a watch room.

A number of weather instruments were installed at the station in 1939, aimed at making weather reports from Montauk "a regular addition to aviation and other weather reporting services.... Reports ... must include scientific reading of all instruments in addition to data concerning height and number of clouds, number of seas breaking on the shore, height of seas, and other information."[32]

In November 1939, it was reported that the station was responsible for 24 major rescues for the year. In addition, the crew had been diligent in the use of its new weather equipment, reporting a high wind of 38 miles per hour, and flying storm warning flags regularly.[33]

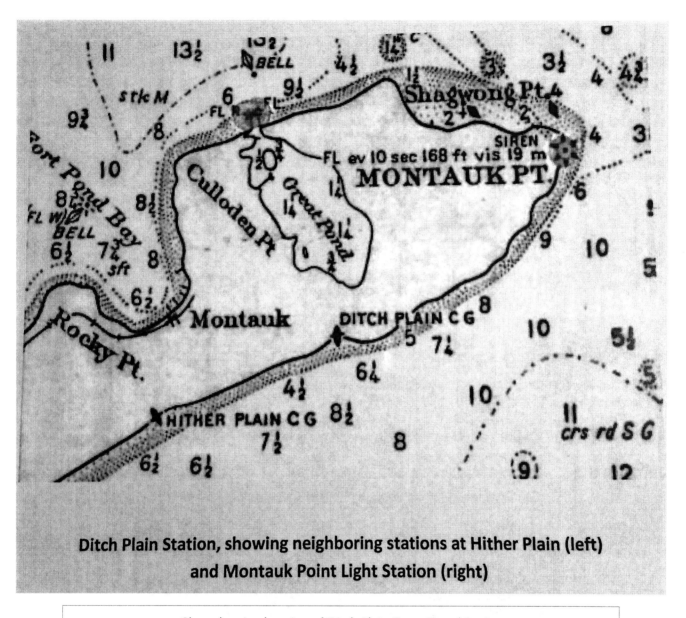

Ditch Plain Station, showing neighboring stations at Hither Plain (left) and Montauk Point Light Station (right)

Chart showing location of Ditch Plain Coast Guard Station. (National Oceanographic and Atmospheric Administration, Office of Coast Survey)

A LEGACY OF VALOR

*The crew and the Lyle Gun appear ready for action in
this 1894 photo at Ditch Plain Life Saving Station.
(Montauk Point Lighthouse Museum)*

During World War II improvements were scheduled for 13 Long Island stations (including Ditch Plain), involving the construction of new barracks at some stations. Plans included new equipment for the building, repairs to the dwelling, and grading the property. The station operated three types of rescue boats during the 1940s. A motor surfboat was kept in a boathouse. A 38-foot picket boat and a 36-foot motor lifeboat were maintained on buoys in Lake Montauk.

In the 1940s and 1950s Ditch Plain Station relied on a patrol cutter from Base 4, New London, for long-range search-and-rescue work, which would often dock at the Montauk Yacht Club or anchor in Lake Montauk.

Patrol craft were not assigned to Montauk until 1962.

The station remained active into the 1950s, some of its buildings and personnel being relocated to Star Island as part of the newly formed Coast Guard Station Montauk in 1955. The Ditch Plain location disappeared from the active list in January 1956. That year the site was turned over to the General Services Administration.

The main station building was eventually moved to a site on Benson Drive in Montauk where it is in private hands. The former station site is now part of Rheinstein Park.

Captains

Patrick Gould (1799-1879), of East Hampton, was appointed keeper of the Montauk Point Lighthouse on May 9, 1832. He served in that capacity until John Hobart replaced him in October 1849. Gould was stationed at the Ditch Plain Life Saving Station, probably from 1855. While there, on December 14, 1856, he was instrumental in rescuing the crew of the brig *Flying Cloud* about three miles west of the lighthouse. He was awarded a gold medal for heroism by the Lifesaving Benevolent Association of New York. His tour of duty at Ditch Plain ended on April 1, 1859. He was also a proprietor of Third House on Montauk in the 1850s where he and his wife had a fine reputation for providing shelter and hospitality to visitors.

Samuel T. Stratton (1824-1894) lived at East Hampton and Montauk. He served as keeper from 1872 to 1877. Like Patrick Gould, Stratton was a proprietor of Third House from the 1850s until 1885. He and his wife kept a guest book which contains names, poems, and anecdotes from contented visitors over the years.

Joshua Edwards, a surfman at Ditch Plain, had issues with Superintendent Henry Huntting, who requested that Edwards remain and take over the station and a newly appointed crew after removal of the former crew for political reasons. Wrote Edwards:

Ditch Plain Coast Guard Station, September 20, 1921
Note the numerous outbuildings at left.
(U.S. Coast Guard)

...the crew...Huntting had appointed was so much inferior to those discharged that he [Edwards] would not take the responsibility and informed said Huntting of the fact; And this deponent further says that he informed said Huntting that he was discharging men from the crews that could not be duplicated as to experience and efficiency; And this deponent further saith that he knows of his own knowledge that said Huntting has caused to be appointed and retained men who are unfit for the position of Life Saving Surfmen for want of experience, efficiency and courage. And..Stratton, Keeper of said Station...did protest, resent, and resist the unwarrantable act of said Huntting in discharging one of the best crews for surf boating on the coast of Long Island.[34]

Frank S. Stratton, a son of Samuel (1856-1931), was appointed keeper on October 9, 1880. He resigned September 20, 1892, and went into the grocery business, which he purchased from A. M. Payne.

*The crew stands at attention at the
Ditch Plain Coast Guard Station in 1941.
(Milton Miller)*

Captain William B. Miller (1840-1909) was born at Amagansett and appointed keeper September 16, 1892. He served in the 127th N.Y. Regiment during the Civil War. In addition to being keeper at Ditch Plain, he served as surfman at the Amagansett station for a number of years. He resigned as keeper for physical reasons on December 2, 1903.

Carl H. Hedges (1857-1938), born at Sagaponack, Long Island, and formerly of the Mecox station near Bridgehampton, became keeper November 28, 1903. He retired due to incapacitation on August 15, 1916.

Warrant Boatswain Russell Garfield Miller (1881-1957), of Springs, served as acting keeper during World War I (1916-1918).

Warrant Boatswain Knowles Smith (1889-1978), of Amagansett, was appointed keeper November 20, 1918, serving until his retirement on February 25, 1924. In 1914 he and his wife opened the Wyandank Restaurant in Montauk. In the 1930s they operated the Wyandannee Inn, which stood near the end of the Old Montauk Highway near the Montauk Point Lighthouse.

Less than a week after Smith's departure, Chief Boatswain's Mate Frank D. Warner (1881-1948) took over, having been transferred from the Quogue Coast Guard Station on Long Island. As a surfman at Quogue, Warner and a fellow station member received the Gold Lifesaving Medal for heroism in the rescue of a sailor aboard the four-masted schooner *Augustus Hunt*, which went down off Quogue on January 22, 1904.

In August 1929, two members of his crew, Oscar Deneuie and Sylvester Beacham, apparently suffering the ill effects of alcohol, attempted to assault Captain Warner, threatening him with a gun and other weapons. They were arrested by police and sent to the Brooklyn Navy Yard for trial. Though they both had good records, Warner felt that they acted as they did because of the "influence of liquor … and acted in such a way as to make him believe they had been drinking rum of a poisonous nature." Warner believed the source of the rum was from the "vicinity of Montauk village."[35] While stationed at Ditch Plain, Captain Warner was one of three Coast Guard officers who later admitted that it was virtually impossible to "stem the liquor flow into Long Island"[36] during the Prohibition era.

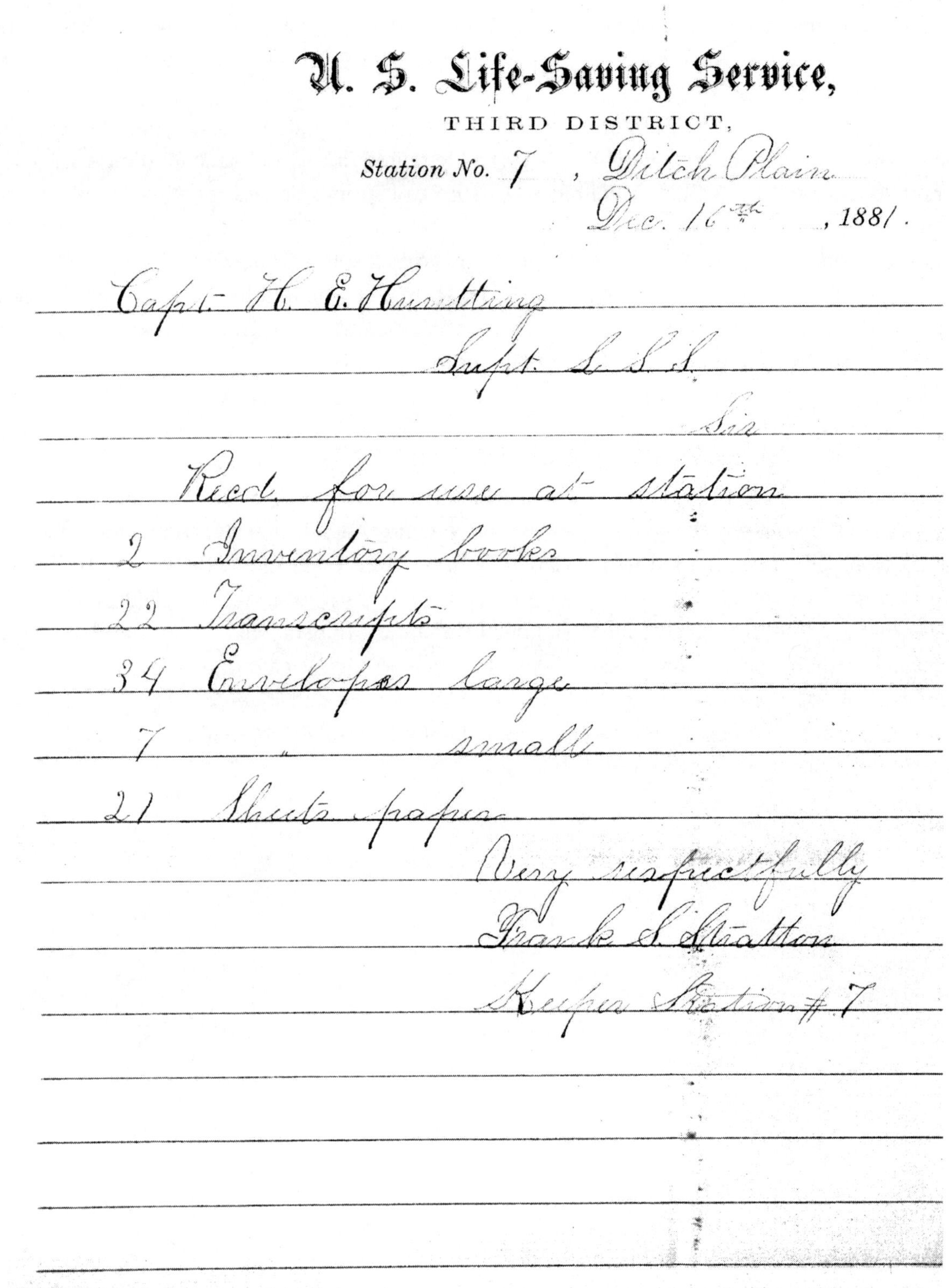

U. S. Life-Saving Service,
THIRD DISTRICT,

Station No. 7, Ditch Plain

Dec. 16th, 1881.

Capt. H. E. Huntting
   Supt. L.S.S.

      Sir

Rec'd for use at station

2 Inventory books
22 Transcripts
34 Envelopes large
7   "   small
21 Sheets paper

Very respectfully
Frank S. Stratton
Keeper Station # 7

Stationery items requested for the Ditch Plain Station, December 16, 1881.
(Henry Huntting Collection — Long Island Collection, East Hampton Library)

| U. S. LIFE-SAVING SERVICE. |
| Form 5. |

REQUISITION.

Superintendent's Office
Bridgehampton N.Y.
September 21st, 1874.

To Hon. B. H. Bristow,
Secretary of the Treasury:

There are required for the use of Station No. 5, District No. 3, Coast of N.Y. & R.I., the following articles, the same being necessary for the public service:

4 Tons Coal at Sag Harbor $8.75	35.00
Transportation	23.33
Fire Brick $2.00, Fire Plates $3.00	5.00
Spun Yarn & Tackle	.75
Repairs on Meter	2.50
	$66.58

Very respectfully, H. E. Huntting
Superintendent.

Approved: J. H. Merryman
Inspector.

Received, _____, 187_, the above-named articles in good order and condition, for use at Station No. _____

Samuel T. Stratton
Keeper.

Supply request for the Ditch Plain Station, September 21, 1874
(Henry Huntting Collection — Long Island Collection, East Hampton Library)

◄ A LEGACY OF VALOR

*Surfman Frank D. Warner in 1905 at Quogue Life Saving Station.
Warner received a Gold Lifesaving Medal after rescuing a
sailor from the doomed schooner Augustus Hunt in 1904.
(Quogue Life Saving Station)*

In October 1930, Captain Warner was promoted to warrant officer. A dinner was held in his honor at the Elks Club in Patchogue. Warner, "is reticent about his honors but at times can be persuaded to show the large solid gold medal [from the 1904 *Augustus Hunt* rescue] and the thrilling recitation of the events in this saga of the sea, as recounted in the official act of Congress, which awarded him the reward."[37]

Captain Warner was transferred to the Point o' Woods Coast Guard Station on Fire Island in March 1931. He was replaced by Chief Boatswain's Mate Lloyd Starrin, who served until 1934. Then Chief Boatswain's Mate Earl M. Pike (1906-?) was in charge of the station. He later served with the U. S. Navy during World War II.

In 1937, Warrant Boatswain John M. Odin (1902-1993) was appointed as the officer in charge, replaced by Chief Boatswain's Mate Charles W. O'Neil in 1939, who served until 1945.

*Captain Frank D. Warner at Ditch Plain Coast Guard
Station, Montauk, in 1935
(Quogue Life Saving Station)*

U. S. LIFE-SAVING SERVICE,
Form 2.

ARTICLES OF ENGAGEMENT FOR SURFMEN.

WE, the subscribers, do, and each of us doth, hereby agree to and with _Samuel T Stratton_, Keeper of Life-Saving Station No. _5_, on the Coast of _New York_, and in the Life-Saving Service of the United States, in manner and form following, that is to say:

In the *first place*, we do hereby agree, in consideration of the monthly wages against each of our names hereunto set, payable at such times and in such proportions as are or may be prescribed by the Secretary of the Treasury of the United States, to enter into the Life-Saving Service of the United States, for the term of one year unless sooner discharged by the order of the Secretary of the Treasury, and to repair to Station No. _5_, on the Coast of _New York_, by the 1st of December, 18_74_ and remain there for four months, that is to say, during the months of December, 18_74_, and January, February, and March, 18_75_ or in due and seasonable time after the date of our engagement, to remain until the 1st day of April, 18_75_ and during that time, unless sooner discharged by proper authority, to the utmost of our power and ability, respectively, to discharge our several duties, and in everything to be conformable and obedient to the lawful commands of the officers who may, from time to time, be placed over us.

Secondly. We do, also, oblige and subject ourselves, and for that purpose do hereby covenant and agree to serve during the term aforesaid, and to comply with and be subject to such rules and discipline as are or may be established for the government of the Life-Saving Service of the United States.

Thirdly. The said _Superintendent_, for and in behalf of the United States, doth hereby covenant and agree to and with the parties who have hereunto severally signed their names, and each of them, respectively, that the said parties shall be paid in consideration of their services, the amount per month which, in the column hereunto annexed, is set opposite to each of their names, respectively, at such times and in such proportions as are or may be allowed by the General Instructions for the government of the Life-Saving Service.

NAMES.	DATE OF ENTRY.	TERM.	IN WHAT CAPACITY.	PAY PER MONTH.		REMARKS.
				Dollars.	Cts.	
William B. Miller	Dec. 1st 1874	4 Mo.	Surfmen	40	—	
Orrin L Roser	"	"	"	40	—	
Elias R Payne	"	"	"	40	—	
William A Baker	"	"	"	40	—	
Chas Fisher	"	"	"	40	—	
Pulaski R Bennett	"	"	"	40	—	

Articles of Engagement for Surfmen at Ditch Plain Station, from December 1, 1874, to March 18, 1875.
(Henry Huntting Collection — Long Island Collection, East Hampton Library)

Form No. 10.

UNITED STATES LIFE-SAVING SERVICE.

District No. 2   Station No. 4

VOUCHER FOR SERVICES AND TRAVELLING EXPENSES, ATTENDING DRILL AND EXERCISE.

We, the subscribers, acknowledge to have received from Henry E. Huntting Superintendent of Life-Saving Stations in District No. 2, the sums set opposite our respective names, in full compensation for services and for travelling expenses incurred by us in attending Drill and Exercise on July 28th, 1873; and we certify, on honor, that the distances charged for mileage were actually and necessarily travelled on public business upon the date herein specified, and under orders from the Superintendent of the District; and that no part of such travel has been under any free pass on any railway, steamboat, or other conveyance:

HOW EMPLOYED.	Days' Service.	Amount.	Miles Travelled.	Amount.	Total Amount.	SIGNATURES.
Keeper	1	3 00	None		3 00	Samuel D. Stratton
Surfman	1	3 „	26	2 60	5 60	Joshua B. Edwards
"	1	3 „	26	2 60	5 60	Thomas B. Rose
"	1	3 „	26	2 60	5 60	Nelson Loper
"	1	3 „	26	2 60	5 60	Charles B. Edwards
"	1	3 „	26	2 60	5 60	Gabriel B. Edwards
"	1	3 „	26	2 60	5 60	Charles H. Ludlow
					36 60	

I HEREBY CERTIFY that the above services were performed under my orders; that they were necessary and proper; and that the respective amounts have been paid to the persons whose signatures appear above, on this 19th day of February, 1874.

APPROVED:

J. H. Merryman
Inspector.

Henry E. Huntting
Superintendent of District.

The crew at Ditch Plain Station received travel expenses for drill and exercise performed on July 28, 1873.
(Henry Huntting Collection — Long Island Collection, East Hampton Library)

Crew Members

Among the earliest records shows the crew in 1872 consisting of keeper Samuel T. Stratton, and surfmen Joshua B. Edwards, Thomas B. Rose, Abram Loper, Charles B. Edwards, Gabriel B. Edwards, Charles A. Ludlow, all of whom were from Amagansett, a distance of 13 miles from the station.

A member of the Ditch Plain crew, Charles S. Miller, died on August 7, 1895 at the age of 38. He "was thrown from his cart about three and a-half years ago, striking his head on a heap of stones, injuring his spine so badly that he has not been able to do a day's work since, and to which cause he has now succumbed."[38] Miller, as previously mentioned, prevented the destruction of the station in 1888 while, in the process of making rubber cement, the mixture caught fire.

In mid-October, 1898, Life Saving Station superintendent Arthur Dominy completed a tour of all stations from Rockaway to Montauk. At Ditch Plain he noticed a few crew members were sick. One of them, David H. Miller, along with members of this family, had typhoid fever. It was noted that the station was very close to Camp Wikoff, where troops were sent to recover from the effects of diseases contracted in Cuba during the Spanish-American War. Dominy also found Pulaski Bennett of the Napeague Station, and Egbert King of Hither Plain Station, suffering from illnesses.

When crews resumed their duty at Long Island stations in August 1899 the Ditch Plain Station was referred to as being "one of the busiest spots on the coast, as the newspaper headquarters, telegraph offices and camp of the Signal Corps were located quite near the boathouse." It was also noted as being "on the ocean side of the site of Camp Wikoff."[39]

Beginning on December 1, 1897, the "seventh (or winter) man," Phineas Dickinson, went on duty at Ditch Plain.

A humorous incident took place at the station early in 1910. It seems that the regular cook was away for a time and a substitute was brought in to prepare the meals. The crew was particularly fond of currant cake so the cook took great efforts to prepare some. However, he forgot to add shortening, and when the crew sat down to eat:

> ...it was found necessary to call for the 'government hatchet' to cut it with, all the table cutlery having been put out of business. Suck a cake as that one was, was considered to be too great a task for a human being's stomach to be called upon to digest, so it was voted to use the waste, indigestible product for stepping stones across the 'drains' encountered on the patrol beats, known to the crew as 'wooden bridges.'[40]

*Crew members at the Ditch Plain Life Saving Station in 1893.
From left to right, keeper William B. Miller, David H. Miller,
Charles S. Miller, unknown, Worden S. Miller
(East Hampton Library — Long Island Collection)*

In mid-September, 1910, surfman Oliver L. Loper found a small copper globe floating in the water containing a metal flag with the number 10 on it. Upon examination, it was discovered that the globe "had been set adrift by the Wide World Magazine in an effort to chart ocean currents, and offering six guineas to the finder if returned immediately to 7-12 Southampton street, Strand, London, England, W. C., with a photograph and description of locality where the globe was found."[41]

Loper dutifully photographed the object and immediately forwarded it to London. He hoped to collect the fee, which was about $30 in U.S. currency. Loper was a dedicated surfman, retiring in April 1915 after 40 years in the service.

David H. Miller, after completing 30 years in the service, applied and received approval for retirement under Section Three of the Act creating the United States Coast Guard of January 28, 1915. This was the first retirement under this legislation in the Third District of the service.

George Sears was appointed No. 1 surfman at the station in December 1915.

The Coast Guard crew at the station held a reception for "twenty or more of the home people" in January 1917. "The boat room was hung with the large alphabetical flags, commencing with 'A' and ending with 'Z' and the national flags which added not a little to the pleasure of the evening. All enjoyed a good time, there being plenty of refreshments, ice cream being furnished by the station men."[42]

This was probably one of the last festive occasions to be enjoyed at the Montauk stations, the clouds of World War I on the horizon.

In May 1922 a substitute at the station, Carl Vaughan, was lost for 11 hours trying to make his way to the station in thick fog. To make matters worse he "fell into the ditch from which the station derives its name. Vaughan was pretty well used up when he managed to reach the station."[43]

The newly constructed (1934) three-story Ditch Plain Coast Guard building and surrounding structures are shown during World War II. A lookout tower was added to the site as part of coastal protection.
(U.S. Coast Guard)

DITCH PLAIN LIFE SAVING STATION

*Ditch Plain Coast Guard Station is shown on August 16, 1941.
(Margaret Buckridge Bock- Montauk Point Lighthouse Museum)*

*The lookout tower at the Ditch Plain Coast
Guard Station on August 16, 1941.
(Margaret Buckridge Bock- Montauk Point Lighthouse Museum)*

The former Ditch Plain Coast Guard building situated on Benson Drive in Montauk is shown in January 2016. It is now in private hands.
(Author photo)

CHAPTER 4

Hither Plain Life Saving Station

LAND WAS CONVEYED in 1855, and a station building erected in 1872. The site was listed as Station No. 24 among stations on the Long Island coast and noted as a "New Station." The building was enlarged in 1877. Its location was given as "one-half mile southwest of Fort Pond." As early as 1873, a New Bedford pulling surfboat was in use here.

Hither Plain Station was within the First Fuel District of the Life Saving Service. In 1895 the station required ten tons of coal as part of its operation.

A record of boats in 1902 showed the following craft at the station:

Model	Builder	Built	Placed at Station
Surf- Beebe	Frederick Beebe, Greenport	1882	1882
Surf- New Bedford	unknown, New Bedford, MA	1873	1873
Surf (open) Beebe	Frederick Beebe, Greenport	1893	1893
Surf- Monomoy	Frederick Beebe, Greenport	1899	1900[44]

With the creation of the U. S. Coast Guard in 1915, Hither Plain became Station No. 66. During World War I a watch tower was built at the station in the summer of 1917, and in September personnel were armed with navy rifles and revolvers.

A new boathouse, 18 X 36 feet, with a cement floor, was under construction by the station crew and completed the following spring. During the early 1920s the station was relatively inactive, but a new boat for drilling arrived in December 1924. As a means of thwarting the activities of rum-runners during the Prohibition era of the 1920s, the station was ordered reopened and improved in April 1924 as part of a $14 million appropriation to enforce the 18th Amendment.

Arthur Miller (1911-2002), of East Hampton, recalled the station in the 1920s as being:

> *one big building. It held twelve men, no bathroom, outside toilet, no showers or nothing! Kinda life they lived in those days. And they couldn't leave their places without permission. If they wanted to walk across the street to our house to visit, they had to ask the Captain 'Can you go?'*[45]

Plans were announced in June 1931 for the construction of a new four-car garage at the station. However, two years later, the Coast Guard announced plans to close the station as of July 1, 1933, as part of an economy measure, the work to be subsequently covered by neighboring stations at Ditch Plain and Napeague. The station was officially listed as inactive in 1934.

*Hither Plain Coast Guard Station as it appeared in 1934.
The telephone poles at left parallel Old Montauk Highway.
The station was officially inactive at that time and would
remain so until World War II.
(U. S. Coast Guard)*

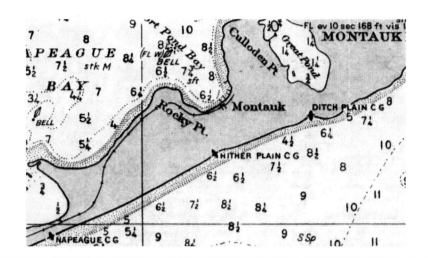

*Chart showing location of Hither Plain Coast Guard Station.
(National Oceanographic and Atmospheric Administration,
Office of Coast Survey)*

In March 1937, citing the need to modernize the Coast Guard's lifesaving capabilities, it was announced that Hither Plain and four other South Shore stations on Long Island would be closed by August 1; the others being at Potunk (Westhampton), Quogue, Tiana, Southampton, and Amagansett. Admiral R. R. Waesche said, "The marked increase in the use of motorboats and radio ... has greatly facilitated life-saving work; and while it has increased the cost of efficient operation of our stations, it has also tended to reduce the need for stations being so close together."[46]

The Hurricane of September 21, 1938, caused significant damage to the station buildings, although the detached boathouse survived and saw use as an auxiliary boathouse to Ditch Plain Station in 1941.

In April 1940 the Coast Guard contemplated razing the station building, replacing it with a new equipment building. In August it was announced that improvements were to be made at 13 Long Island stations, including Hither Plain, where the old station building would be demolished and repairs made to the equipment building.

During World War II the site was used as a Loran station. Meanwhile, across the road (Old Montauk Highway) from the station, the Parsons Inn was renovated into a barracks to accommodate servicemen.[47]

The station was abandoned permanently in 1948 and the buildings razed thereafter. The station stood on the south side of Old Montauk Highway across from Washington Avenue.

Captains

Among the early keepers at Hither Plain was John B. Lawrence (1830-1915). A whaler out of Plymouth, Massachusetts, aboard the brig *Webster*, bound from the Canary Islands with a cargo of nuts, the ship encountered a snowstorm and beached at Amagansett on March 24, 1856. Lawrence settled in Amagansett and was later part of the first crew of the Napeague Life Saving Station. He was known to be stationed at Hither Plain as early as July 1869. He resigned his post in June 1873.

George H. Osborne (1832-1899) was first keeper at Hither Plain. He was appointed keeper December 9, 1872, serving until September 14, 1881. Apparently, he was not viewed as a suitable keeper in a letter by August E. Remington on January 2, 1878:

I have known said Osborn for twenty years or so…having lived in his family as a boarder [at Montauk] and when not so living have been a frequent visitor in his house; that said George Osborn is a man of notoriously intemperate habits. And has been so continuously for the last 20 years…since his appointment as keeper…has been drunk on several occasions lying out in barns for nights and days together. That one year ago this winter of 1878 he started from the village of East Hampton for his home on Montauk, some fifteen miles distant. And brought up on Napeague Beach some five miles from his house so drunk that he could go no further; this in the winter season…

This man has been kept in his place by Supt. Huntting with a full knowledge of his habits as they are notorious. And it is well known that said Osborn is always ready to drink with every Indian who might have a jug of Rum…

…said Osborn was appointed at the instance of said Supt. Huntting knowing that he was not and did not profess to be a surfman capable of handling his boat in the surf in a time of need and danger.

Inventory of Public Property for Station No. 3 (Hither Plain), signed by keeper George H. Osborn on March 31, 1873 (Henry Huntting Collection — Long Island Collection, East Hampton Library)

In the same correspondence, Remington took the opportunity to give his opinion of Superintendent Huntting and how he managed (or mismanaged) the stations of eastern Long Island:

> ...the Life Saving Service for twenty miles westward from Montauk Point has to my own knowledge been made and used as a political machine by the Superintendent thereof to promote the interests of local politicians and hereby protest as a republican of more than twenty years standing against this debasement of the public service to the constant peril of life and property exposed to destruction on the Long Island Coast.[48]

The sense of isolation is evident in this view of the Hither Plain Coast Guard Station.
(Montauk Library)

Jesse Edwards, one of the crewmen also removed at the time, echoed these thoughts but spoke in defense of keeper Osborn: "Keeper George Osborn in the house of this deponent and in the presence of this deponent's family said that he...informed the said Huntting that if he [Osborn] could not select his own crew, he the said Huntting could put in who he was a mind to and that he the said Osborn would not be responsible."[49]

George E. Filer (1839-1908) served from September 14, 1881, until his resignation on November 16, 1891. Routine visits to stations assured the competence of captains and crew members. On July 7, 1882, Charles B. Dayton wrote, "I have personally examined George E. Filer Keeper of U. S. L. S. Station No. 8 and find him able-bodied and healthy in every respect."[50]

In addition to routine equipment at the station, Filer made an unusual request in a letter to Superintendent Huntting on November 13, 1884: "Forms referring to Keeping of horse received, can have horse here by 20th inst."[51]

*A dirigible passes Hither Plain Coast Guard Station ca. 1917.
All Coast Guard stations were on extra alert during World War I.
(Montauk Library)*

William D. Parsons (1860-1940) began his service as keeper on January 25, 1892. He was apparently proficient as a farmer as well. In February 1901 a report noted that during 1900, "he harvested 165 bushels of corn from about three-fifths of an acre, which is said to be a corn record for the east end. Captain Parsons was raised on a farm and he says he has not forgotten how to manage one, even if the best part of his life has been on the water."[52] Parsons was reassigned to the nearby Napeague station on August 1, 1917. Upon his retirement in March 1919 he returned to his home nearly opposite the Hither Plain station where his Parsons Inn "is well patronized during the summer months. One seeking quiet and comfort can do no better than stop at the Parsons house a few weeks."[53]

Sometimes, rescues made by lifesavers occurred on land. Keeper Parsons was involved in an unusual accident in early July 1891. Theodore Stratton of Montauk was driving a team of horses and a wagon over the Montauk hills when the pole strap broke, causing the pole to catch in the ground, bring the wagon to a sudden stop and hurtling Stratton through the air and to the ground, causing serious injury. The horses continued on, only to collide with another wagon that was driven by keeper Parsons. The wild horses rode on and were not found again until late next morning. Parsons realized from the runaway horses that there must have been an accident, found Stratton unconscious, and took him home where he was attended by a Dr. Sterling.

While walking along the east shore of Fort Pond Bay on March 15, 1896, a woman from Montauk discovered a body. When she returned to her village she notified the keeper, Captain Jesse Edwards, of the Amagansett station, who contacted the Hither Plain station. Keeper William Parsons and crew retrieved the body, which they then covered with canvas before notifying the coroner. When the coroner arrived the next day he decided to hold the inquest at Amagansett, so the lifesavers took the body to the Montauk train station to be transported there.

On March 12, 1899, Captain Parsons and his crew at Hither Plain station succeeded in capturing a finback whale. Captain Parsons had been taking weather observations when he spotted a black object in the water. Not realizing what they were headed for, they launched the lifeboat in anticipation of a rescue. Upon approaching, the men realized what they had found. Upon closer examination, Captain Parsons discovered that the whale was dead and efforts were made to drag it onto the beach. Once hauled ashore, it was measured at 58 feet in length, with a tail of 15 feet. Although there was no sign of injury to the mammal, the lifesavers speculated that it may have collided with an ocean liner.

The Hither Plain Coast Guard Station is shown in the 1930s. Old Montauk Highway on the right.
(Montauk Library)

*Testing lifesaving apparatus at the
Hither Plain Coast Guard Station
(Montauk Library)*

The lifesavers anticipated the opportunity to make a profit, since although finback whales have little or no whalebone, they were valuable for the oil.

Next day, Captains Joshua Edwards and Gabriel Edwards, whalers from Amagansett, came to cut up the whale and extract the oil via their tryworks. The yield was twenty barrels of oil, valued at a sizeable $200.

Hiram Francis King (1882-1954) was appointed August 1, 1917, and transferred December 9, 1920. Then the keeper position was vacant for two years, and in 1922 the station was shut down.

It was reactivated in 1925, but the keeper position was still vacant. Chief Boatswain's Mate Jetur Reeve Harlow (1868-1953) was placed in charge in 1928. In May 1930 he was transferred to the Mecox Station at Bridgehampton. Harlow had been well liked while at Montauk, as friends "regret his departure but expect he will visit here frequently."[54]

Being a Navy man, Harlow seemed to pride himself on how efficiently he ran his station and controlled his subordinates. However, according to Charles Frank Miller (1903-1999), on occasion, while he was playing cribbage at the Parsons Inn across Old Montauk Highway from the station, he remarked, "I got them under control. They don't put anything over on me. However, young Miller looked out the window and... saw [the men] come over the roof, down the telephone pole and up over the hill. Goin' to the movies."[55]

Capt. Cecil F. Wessells, formerly of the Mecox Station, was placed in charge at Hither Plain. He was later transferred to the neighboring Napeague Station and in March 1931 to Chincoteague Island, Virginia.

In July 1933, when Earl M. Pike was captain, the station was closed and he was transferred to the neighboring Ditch Plain Station. William Hawley was placed in charge at Hither Plain as a caretaker, previously serving at the Jones Beach Station, Long Island. The station remained inactive until World War II.

Crew Members

The earliest recorded list of crew members (1872) included George H. Osborn, keeper, and surfmen Jesse B. Edwards, Jonathan Edwards, Albert B. Edwards, Daniel B. Loper, Madison F. King, Jonathan E. Payne, and Albert Halsey, all of Amagansett, about 10 miles distant from the station.

Christmas of 1887 was a joyous occasion for two members of the station in particular — William B. Miller and David H. Miller. It was said they were "of course, like little children, very much pleased with their presents which were quite numerous and of a great variety."[56]

Robert J. Collins made sure crew members were eating well when it was reported in January 1887 he was "furnishing the mess table with wild duck."[57]

Egbert King liked fox hunting, and in January 1887 came to the conclusion that they were now scarce on Montauk.

Beginning on December 1, 1897, an additional crewman, known as the "seventh (or winter) man," went on duty at all stations within the district. The new man at Hither Plain was William L. Baker. Baker retired from the station in 1916 after 30 years in the Life Saving Service.

David H. Bennett, who had served in the lifesaving service for 22 years, all at Hither Plain station, died suddenly of pneumonia on August 28, 1905, at the age of 61.

Being a member of the Coast Guard required one to be in good physical condition. To that end, Arthur Miller was sent to the hospital in May 1916 "to have his feet treated," since he "has been a great sufferer for a long time and his many friends wish him a speedy recovery."[58]

U. S. LIFE-SAVING SERVICE,
Form 2.

ARTICLES OF ENGAGEMENT FOR SURFMEN.

WE, the subscribers, do, and each of us doth, hereby agree to and with George H. Osborn, Keeper of Life-Saving Station No. 6, on the Coast of New York, and in the Life-Saving Service of the United States, in manner and form following, that is to say:

In the *first place*, we do hereby agree, in consideration of the monthly wages against each of our names hereunto set, payable at such times and in such proportions as are or may be prescribed by the Secretary of the Treasury of the United States, to enter into the Life-Saving Service of the United States, for the term of one year unless sooner discharged by the order of the Secretary of the Treasury, and to repair to Station No. 6, on the Coast of New York, by the 1st of December, 18 74/, and remain there for four months, that is to say, during the months of December, 18 74/ and January, February, and March, 18 75/, or in due and seasonable time after the date of our engagement, to remain until the 1st day of April, 18 75/, and during that time, unless sooner discharged by proper authority, to the utmost of our power and ability, respectively, to discharge our several duties, and in everything to be conformable and obedient to the lawful commands of the officers who may, from time to time, be placed over us.

Secondly. We do, also, oblige and subject ourselves, and for that purpose do hereby covenant and agree to serve during the term aforesaid, and to comply with and be subject to such rules and discipline as are or may be established for the government of the Life-Saving Service of the United States.

Thirdly. The said Superintendent, for and in behalf of the United States, doth hereby covenant and agree to and with the parties who have hereunto severally signed their names, and each of them, respectively, that the said parties shall be paid in consideration of their services, the amount per month which, in the column hereunto annexed, is set opposite to each of their names, respectively, at such times and in such proportions as are or may be allowed by the General Instructions for the government of the Life-Saving Service.

NAMES.	DATE OF ENTRY.	TERM.	IN WHAT CAPACITY.	Pay per Month.		REMARKS.
				Dollars.	Cts.	
David C. Miller	Dec 1st 1874	4 Mo	Surfman	40	—	
Daniel B. Leper	"	"	"	40	—	
George G. Miller	"	"	"	40	—	
William B. Bailey	"	"	"	40	—	
Albert M. Payne	"	"	"	40	—	
Erastus B. Eck	"	"	"	40	—	

*Articles of Engagement for Surfmen at Hither Plain Station,
from December 1, 1874, to March 18, 1875.
(Henry Huntting Collection — Long Island Collection, East Hampton Library)*

The crew at Hither Plain Station received travel expenses for drill and exercise performed on July 28, 1873.
(Henry Huntting Collection — Long Island Collection, East Hampton Library)

*A postcard view of Hither Plain Life Saving Station.
The caption reads "N. M. Tuthill Post Cards."
(U. S. Coast Guard)*

*To reach the Hither Plain Coast Guard Station in
1924 one had to take Old Montauk Highway,
a dirt road at that time.
(Queens Borough Public Library, Long Island Division,
Eugene L. Armbruster Photographs)*

Old Montauk Highway in January 2016 shows the same view as above. The wooded area to the right of the truck is the former site of the Hither Plain Station.
(Author photo)

The description for this image reads, "A display of the International Code Flags used by the U. S. Gov't in the Coast Guard Stations. Coast Guard Station 66. August 15, 1919."
This was at the Hither Plain Station.
(Montauk Library)

HITHER PLAIN LIFE SAVING STATION

*Buildings at the Hither Plain Coast Guard Station during World War II. The site suffered much damage after the 1938 Hurricane.
(U. S. Coast Guard)*

CHAPTER 5

U. S. Coast Guard Station Montauk

THE U. S. Coast Guard is a combination of five former federal agencies: Revenue Cutter Service, Life Saving Service, Steamboat Inspection Service, Bureau of Navigation, and the Lighthouse Service, which was the last to be absorbed in 1939.

In March 1917 Coast Guard crews were under strict rules and drills in order to be prepared in the event of war. At the onset of World War I, all stations were placed under the control of the U.S. Navy. Unlike previous years when stations were unmanned during summer months, crews at Montauk stations and elsewhere began year-round duty. In July 1917 watch towers were ready for use at the Ditch Plain and Hither Plain stations, and by September all crew members were armed with rifles and revolvers while on patrols.

In March 1918 Joseph Meade, keeper at Ditch Plain Station, and Hiram King of Hither Plain Station were appointed to the newly created positions of military inspector in the Coast Guard. A total of three inspectors were appointed for the Long Island District. They visited each station and instructed crews in the proper use of firearms that had recently been issued.

Changes in equipment and technology over the years spelled doom for the many stations in the Coast Guard system. The introduction of motorized lifeboats, air patrols, and radio communications made it easier to patrol larger areas, thereby eliminating the need for many existing stations. Consolidations and closings were considered, though some stations that had been shut down prior to World War II were reopened as part of coastal defense.

Following the war, closings began in earnest. In particular, the perfection of radio-direction-finding made it easier for ships to navigate clear of danger areas, and radar and sonar techniques were improved. Even helicopters became part of equipment.

The conducting of beach patrols, so significant during World War II, basically came to an end by 1951 with the advent of new technology. "Radar, loran, improved communications including radio telephones on small craft, search and rescue by airplanes, and the use of amphibious vehicles have crowded out the lonely watcher who used to tramp sandy miles and strain eyes seaward."[59] By this time, stations at Georgica and Napeague had been closed and equipment removed, and the former Hither Plain Station demolished. In addition to Ditch Plain, only six other stations remained active on Long Island, with the nearest station to Montauk being at Shinnecock (Hampton Bays), 35 miles to the west.

With the changing patterns of marine traffic in the vicinity of Montauk, it was found to be more effective to maintain station boats at recently leased property on Star Island in Lake Montauk, and negotiations were under way to acquire additional land in preparation for relocating the Coast Guard station there from Ditch Plain.

Napeague Coast Guard Station shown after the
Hurricane of September 21, 1938. The station was
active during World War II but was closed by 1948.
(U. S. Coast Guard)

Napeague Coast Guard Station is prepared for its
move to Star Island in Lake Montauk, 1954.
(Montauk Library)

*Mounted on a barge, the former Napeague Coast Guard Station is on its way to its new home on Star Island in Lake Montauk, 1954.
(East Hampton Library, Long Island Collection)*

*Relocation of Napeague Coast Guard Station to
Star Island in Lake Montauk, March 1955.
The structure was towed 10 miles to become headquarters
for new Coast Guard Station Montauk.
(East Hampton Library, Long Island Collection)*

By May 1952 a permanent rescue station was established at Star Island. Its equipment included an 83-foot patrol boat. At that time plans were in progress to move two structures from the Ditch Plain Station and the main building from the former Napeague Coast Guard Station to Star Island. Meanwhile, the patrol boat, a lifeboat, and picket boat were to be docked temporarily at the Montauk Yacht Club.

In November 1954 it was announced that the Napeague Station building would be hauled 10 miles by barge through Napeague Harbor and Gardiner's Bay to Star Island, and the new site named the Montauk Life Boat Station. In the process of relocating the structure, it was blown aground during a winter storm while still in Napeague Harbor. Weather conditions and obstruction from power lines also delayed the process at least six weeks. Finally, in mid-March 1955, the 3-story, 15-room building arrived at its new home. The process of consolidating Coast Guard stations at Montauk was now complete.

What came to be known as Coast Guard Station Montauk was officially commissioned on October 1, 1955. It became part of Moriches Group, which also included stations at Shinnecock and Moriches. Around that time a flag-raising ceremony and an open house were held. The crew of 15 was ready to furnish additional protection for the increased boating activity around Montauk.

The station was equipped with a type TRS motor lifeboat and a Cabin Picket Boat. In November 1965 a new 44-foot lifeboat, CG-44348, arrived at the station. It supplemented search and rescue and law enforcement capability of the Coast Guard in the Montauk area. Especially designed for search and rescue work, it had a self-righting capability if capsized, and a double bottom in the event of grounding and ice-working damage.[60]

Patrol craft was permanently assigned to the station in 1963 with the arrival of the 82-foot WPB *Point Wells*. Changes in craft occurred several times over the years. In 2012 the station contained two 47-foot motor lifeboats CG47279 and CG 47301, plus a 25-foot, small Response Boat CG25540.

On March 23, 2001, the *Point Wells* was replaced by the newly-commissioned, 87-foot cutter *Ripley*, the same crew transferring from the old ship to the new. In the summer of 2016, the Ripley was replaced by another 87-foot cutter, the Bonito.

On October 3, 2005, the main building at the station was dedicated as Bruckenthal Hall, in honor of Petty Officer 3rd Class Nathan B. Bruckenthal, who, at the young age of 24, was killed in the line of duty in Iraq on April 24, 2004. At the time of the dedication, he was the first Coast Guardsman killed in action since the Vietnam War. He was buried in Arlington National Cemetery.

The station underwent massive renovation in 2007-2008, with the rebuilding of the Administration and garage buildings, and an addition to the garage building to house the boatswain's mate's shop.

Today, Station Montauk is part of Coast Guard Sector Long Island Sound, established on May 31, 2005, within the First Coast Guard District of the United States. Boatswain's Mate Senior Chief Petty Officer Eric Best is in charge of the station, appointed in June 2015.

Coast Guard Station Montauk, January 2016.
The Montauk Peninsula saw much activity in the days
of the old Life Saving Service and early Coast Guard years.
With modern technology the station is able to respond more
rapidly and efficiently to maritime disasters and mishaps at sea.
(Author Photo)

CHAPTER 6

Notable Shipwrecks 1600s – 1877
Prior to the formation of the U. S. Life Saving Service

DURING THE 18TH century on Long Island, increasing numbers of ships sailed from England and France to the fledgling port of New York, many of them passing Montauk Point along the way. Without the guiding flame from the lantern of a lighthouse these vessels often risked death and destruction when sailing too near the rocky shores of Montauk. Consequently, a number of captains voiced the need for a lighthouse at Montauk Point.

In 1796 New York's first lighthouse was constructed at Montauk Point. Once in operation, its guiding light caused a sharp decline in the number of shipwrecks along the shores of Montauk and eastern Long Island.

During these years sailing ships dominated the seas, noting landmarks along the shores, such as the Montauk Lighthouse, to guide them. Though these ships did not require fuel or machinery to propel them, the advance of steam-powered vessels brought speed and the ability to navigate without being affected by winds. During this Age of Sail, and just prior to the organization of the U. S. Life Saving Service in 1878, some interesting maritime disasters occurred along the shores of Montauk.

John & Lucy (1668)

The earliest recorded nautical mishap that occurred at Montauk was that of the *John & Lucy*, which set sail from Rhode Island for Long Island on February 10, 1668, but shifting wind patterns caused a change in plans and the ship headed for New London. About an hour and a half later, about three miles from Fishers Island, the *John & Lucy* "struck fast upon a Rock, where she did beat all the night long."

The crew grew fearful and confused as to what to do next. The chief mate, John Jennings, did not inspire confidence as he "did put on all the clothes he could well put on which was a great discouragement to all the rest." This was followed by second mate Daniel Gibbs doing likewise, instilling "this great fear wherein the Master would be not regarded nor obeyed."

In general, there was a "terrible distraction and confusion in the ship all the night long, one ergine [sic] this the other that, doing one thing and then undoing it, doing all things and yet nothing … and at break of day the ship beating so extremely that…all courage was taken away, and as sudainly … the boates were full of men."[61]

Only three men remained aboard the *John & Lucy*, which floated with high tide and grounded "upon this shoare of Montauket, where the ship stuck fast & still lieth." The three men came ashore where they were encouraged by East Hampton Town Constable Thomas Baker to go to town for care, but one of the men, Thomas Jones, refused, claiming he "had charge of the Master's goods which he would not forsake."[62]

Mary (1701)

In colonial times the British forbade commerce "with foreign plantations," and, according to Jeannette Edwards Rattray, "up until 1763 trade with Canada had to take the form of smuggling, but there was plenty of it."[63] Involved in such activity was the sloop *Mary*, which wrecked at Montauk on November 23, 1701. It had previously carried cheese, flour, tobacco, and shot from New York to Canada and was now carrying brandy, claret, wine, furs, cotton goods, and beads from Quebec on the return trip.

Apparently no one was aboard when the ship went ashore. Capt. Josiah Hobart, Justice of the Peace of the Town of East Hampton, and Abraham Schellinger (1658-1711), a ship owner, condemned the vessel and cargo for violation of trade and navigation laws.

When the revenue officers came they faced problems. Several prominent local residents were listed in a journal titled, "Names of men that watched the goods upon the Beatch att Menatauke Belonging to the Sloop Mary," and those who carted away the goods. Nobody could account for many of the items such as barrels of brandy, cloth, and other things that people "did bair away into the woods."[64]

H.M.S. Culloden (1781)

During the American Revolution, the British took control of Long Island following a victory at Brooklyn on August 27, 1776. This increased the possibility of raids on cattle grazing at Montauk. The British maintained a fleet in Gardiner's Bay and one ship in an area thought to be Fort Pond Bay, Montauk. Among their ships stationed there in September 1780 was the *Culloden*, which contained 74 guns, was 170 feet long, 47 feet wide, had three decks and a crew of about 650. The *Culloden* was considered the fastest and most powerful vessel of the squadron at Gardiner's Bay, and had been declared "invincible" by British authorities.

The wreck of this ship on January 23, 1781, is recalled in *American Gibraltar: Montauk and the Wars of America*:

> *When three French ships were seen off Newport, Rhode Island moving toward Long Island, presumably to aid the American cause, the order was given for the Culloden and two other ships—the Bedford and the America—to chase them off. However, a blinding snowstorm moved in and the ships made an attempt to head for the open sea. The Bedford and America made it to safety but the Culloden struck at Shagwong Reef near Montauk Point, opening a hole in its hull. The ship attempted to reach calmer waters in Fort Pond Bay but ran aground off what was then known as Will's (now Culloden) Point. Attempts to refloat the vessel were fruitless. To prevent the Americans from salvaging the ship's guns, the British burned the vessel to the waterline, taking what they could with them. There were no casualties.*[65]

The safe evacuation of everyone aboard was due, "according to a British report, to the fine discipline maintained. The several hundred men were drawn up in line and marched forward, dropping one by one from the tip of the bowsprit to the shallow water beneath." The same report said that the loss of the *Culloden* was a "severe blow to British morale and certainly contributed to ultimate British defeat."[66]

In the spring of 1782, after the British had left Long Island, Joseph Woodbridge of Groton, Connecticut, salvaged 16 of the cannons from the sunken ship and offered to sell them to Gen. George Washington. However, the army did not have the money and could not afford them. What happened to these guns is unknown.[67]

In 1885 it was reported that after having been buried under the sand for years, signs of the wreckage were becoming visible at low tide. Parts of wreckage from the ship, visible for years at Culloden Point, were found in 1971. After subsequent years of attempts among divers and scientists to salvage artifacts and to raise the vessel, the wreck site was placed on the National Register of Historic Places, allowing it to remain safely at rest.

H.M.S. Culloden in its sailing days. Once aground at Montauk, all 74 of its guns and more than 600 men were safely removed from the vessel by its British crew.
(Montauk Point Lighthouse Museum)

A model of the Culloden, built by Anthony Pagan of Center Moriches, New York, is shown on display at the Montauk Point Lighthouse Museum, February 2016. (Author photo)

Peggy (1786)

On November 18, 1786, the 50-ton brig, *Peggy*, captained by Thomas Thompson and bound for Rhode Island from Bermuda, wrecked at Montauk in a severe snowstorm. Seven of the ten aboard were lost.

The *Peggy* was built at Bermuda in 1784 and registered there by its owner, Theodore Godet, a man of influence who helped protect the island from French privateers. The *Peggy* sailed frequently to America and the West Indies, carrying bread, pork, corn, flour, rice, and onions. [68]

Friendship (1810)

The brig *Friendship*, sailing from Boston to Wilmington, sprang a leak and ran aground at Montauk on March 21, 1810. Cargo consisted of rum, sugar, paints, brick, oars, leather, and pleasure wagons.

Orion (1815)

In a letter dated September 24, 1815, from A. M. Smith to New York State customs officer Henry Packer Dering (1763-1822), Smith writes that a "Brigg from Petersburg, cargo Hemp and iron, was yesterday stranded at Montauk. The Vessel, I am informed, is entirely lost, and of the cargo, they expect to save only a small portion of the iron. I have no opportunity to obtain further information."

The ship, bound for Providence, went down in a great hurricane the day before. The crew was saved, as were the 200 tons of iron. The hurricane was strong enough to put the Montauk Point Lighthouse out of service for a time.

Ligera (1823)

The loss of the Spanish schooner *Ligera* was a mystery. Sailing from Havana to New York with a cargo of fruit and specie (coined money), it went down at Shagwong Reef on the night of December 6, 1823. Ten men, including the captain, came ashore with what was thought to be about $20,000. Later, a boat set out to remove the remaining seven crew members from the wrecked ship, but it was not found. The next morning, the ship's masts and topsails were seen offshore.

The weather on the day of the wreck was "calm, or very little wind, and smooth water. How seven men could be drowned in such a situation, with the vessel's masts and top sails yards above water, and not three miles from the shore, is somewhat extraordinary!"[69]

Soon after, it was reported that the *Ligera* came ashore, and two boxes of oranges were sent to the Customs House in Sag Harbor.

Susan (1826)

The schooner *Susan* of Machias, Maine, bound to Providence from Savannah with a cargo of cotton, was struck by lightning on the evening of March 20, 1826, about 100 miles off Montauk Point, igniting cotton, "and every exertion made to stifle the fire, and by throwing water down the after sky-light to extinguish it, but to no purpose."[70] The fire destroyed the ability to navigate the vessel properly, and it drifted to Montauk shores about a day and half later where the deck collapsed and the ship burned to the water's edge. One hundred of the 300 bales of cotton were salvaged, and all aboard were saved.

Triumph (1835)

On May 29, 1835, the brig *Triumph* under Captain Prior, came ashore 10 miles west of the Montauk Lighthouse. All aboard were safe, as was the cargo of cotton and staves (wooden posts or planks).

Edward Quesnel (1839)

The ship *Edward Quesnel*, carrying 2,300 barrels of whale oil, ran aground at Napeague on the night of May 13, 1839, and quickly broke apart. The second mate and six members of the crew drowned while attempting to land. By the end of the month it was reported that the remainder of the bodies had been recovered.

Henry P. Hedges (1817-1911), East Hampton historian, recalled the grisly event years later:[71]

The bodies were drawn up on the beach near the banks. A ghastly array of corpses, pitiful to behold. The mortal blow leaves on the lifeless body that mark which appalls the onlooker even in the home where it fell. On the wild ocean, or its wild shore, the surging billows, the grinding and groaning wreck, the crash of breaking cargo, the desolation of the scene adds four-fold to the desolating horror of death. That vision of lifeless bodies lying in a row on Napeague beach, pale, motionless, ghastly, has followed and haunted me in the darkness of night from that day to this.

Plato (1842)

The bark *Plato*, bound for New Bedford from the Indian Ocean with 1,600 barrels of whale oil and bone, went ashore ten miles west of the Montauk Lighthouse on October 14, 1842. Five seamen were lost, four of whom were buried at the burial grounds at Montauk. Most of cargo was saved, but the ship was a total loss.

The vessel was insured with four companies: New Bedford Commercial Office, $10,000; Fairhaven Insurance Office, $10,000; Sun Mutual Office, New York, $8,000, and Mutual Safety Insurance Office, New York, $8,000.[72]

Julia (1848)

The schooner *Julia*, of Portland, Maine, bound from Richmond, Virginia, for Portland with a cargo of coal, came ashore in a heavy gale about 10 miles west of the Montauk Light in March, 1848. The crew was rescued, but the ship and cargo of coal were a total loss.

Olga (1850)

On May 6, 1850, the British bark *Olga*, bound from Sunderland, England, to New Haven with a cargo of coal, grounded in heavy fog nine miles west of the Lighthouse. All aboard were rescued.

Marcellus (1852)

On the evening of April 18, 1852, the brig *Marcellus*, Captain Thomas, from Puerto Rico, bound for New Haven with a cargo of molasses, went aground south of Fort Pond. Two men were lost, Timothy James, seaman, and Peter Ernos, cook. "The rest of the crew were nearly exhausted when drawn on shore by the means of a rope which they succeeded in getting ashore for the brig."[73] The cargo was considered lost.

Nantucket Lightship #11 (1855)

Nantucket Shoals, located about 100 miles southeast of Cape Cod, Massachusetts, was one of the most remote lightship station sites in the world. Since the lightship marked the turning point on the trans-Atlantic sea lane for ships between Europe and the United States, for 130 years (1854-1983) twelve different lightships were assigned to warn of this treacherous hazard to navigation. The first was the *Nantucket LV-11*, placed in service in 1854.

A common threat to lightships maintaining their station was vulnerability to severe weather conditions.

At Nantucket Shoals, lightships were blown off station no fewer than 33 times in history, and on February 5, 1855, the *LV-11* lost its anchorage. The ship actually drifted all the way to Montauk Point, a distance of 113 nautical miles, running aground about a mile and a half west of the Montauk Lighthouse on February 8. The crew was safe but the vessel was described "at present tight, but in a very critical situation."[74] It was later salvaged and rebuilt at the New York Navy Yard at a cost of $11,000, and assigned to duty as the Scotland Lightship off New York.

Flying Cloud
Wrecked at Montauk in December 1856. Patrick Gould received
a gold medal from the Life Saving Benevolent Association
for his efforts in rescuing its crew.

Flying Cloud (1856)

The brig *Flying Cloud*, of Bangor, Maine, sailing from Philadelphia and bound for Charlestown, Massachusetts, with 276 tons of coal, ran aground in a storm about three miles west of the Montauk

Lighthouse on December 14, 1856. The ship was a total loss, but Capt. Edmund Chase and his crew were rescued by Capt. Patrick Gould of the Ditch Plain Life Saving Station, who sent a line out to the ship via a rocket. Montauk Lighthouse keeper Jason Terbell (1809-1882) was also involved in the rescue operation.

Captain Chase expressed his gratitude to Gould for his efforts in a letter to the Sag Harbor *Corrector*:

> *The storm at the time we struck was very severe, a heavy sea broke over us continually. We were wet through. The crew of the Station House saw us, and hastened to our relief, and all, particularly Mr. Gould, the keeper, and Wreckmaster Terbell, were indefatigable in their exertions to assist us. The Station House was distant more than a mile, but notwithstanding this, and the rain, and the storm, they made a number of trips to procure means for our rescue...*
>
> *Our escape is owing solely to the humanity and liberality of our Government, in thus providing for wrecked mariners. These Life Stations are just what should be, and in my opinion, are the best means to save life and property that ever can, or will be projected. I appreciate them highly, and if the crews of all the stations labor as faithfully at such times, as those at Montauk, very little if any lives or property will ever be lost on the coast of this Island.*
>
> *I shall never cease to remember Messrs. Gould and Terbell and shall consider myself able to discharge any indebtedness to them. Myself and Crew lost all our clothing and every thing, but by the hospitality and kindness of Mr. and Mrs. Gould, after we reached their house were provided with every thing to make us comfortable. I trust if I am ever wrecked again I shall fall in as kind and good hands.*[75]

In January 1857, Captain Gould was presented with a gold medal from the Life Saving Benevolent Association of New York for his efforts in rescuing the crew. It was inscribed as follows:

> *Vita Feliciter Ausis Servata**
> *Presented, January 1857 to Patrick T. Gould, for his*
> *courage and humanity in saving from inevitable death*
> *the crew of the brig Flying Cloud, wrecked on*
> *Montauk Point, L. I., December 14, 1856."*

A visitor to Montauk, Charles Lanman, wrote of Captain Gould:

> *Of this worthy man I would further remark that he was born in East Hampton, spent his early life as a carpenter in New York city, was keeper of the Montauk Light for seventeen and a half years, and keeper also for nine years of the Herdsmen's House at Indian Fields (now Third House), where I formed his acquaintance and that of his interesting family; and at the present time leading, in the seventy-first year of his age, the peaceful life of a farmer on the outskirts of East Hampton.*[76]

John Milton (1858)

One of Montauk's most famous maritime disasters was the wreck of the clipper *John Milton* on February 20, 1858. Considered "one of the most beautiful ships afloat,"[77] the *John Milton* was launched from New Bedford, Massachusetts, on October 7, 1854. A few months later it sailed to San Francisco, arriving on July 14, 1855.

On December 6, 1856 the ship departed New York with Captain Ephraim Harding at the helm. It arrived in San Francisco on May 6, 1857, and remained there for more than a month. This was not unusual, because in those days "many a ship's crew abandoned their vessels entirely upon arrival in San Francisco and struck out for the California hills in a frenzied search for gold. As a result, the ships stood silently in the bay, eventually being broken up by enterprising citizens who used the material to create new landfill for additional construction."[78]

Captain Harding assembled a crew from the city and sailed on June 12, making a stop at the Chincha Islands off Peru to take on a cargo of guano, which was used as fertilizer by farmers. The destination was New Bedford.

On February 13, 1858, as the *John Milton* made its way up the Eastern Seaboard of the United States, a severe storm was building, complete with high winds, blinding snow, and rough seas. Navigation became increasingly difficult as the ship made its way slowly toward Long Island, eventually changing to an eastern course along the island's South Shore.

The coast of Montauk at that time was described by one reporter as "exceedingly bleak and desolate … [having] more the appearance of a barren wilderness than a settled and civilized country, and is entirely unsheltered from the elements. During a storm the sea breaks with terrible fury on the beach, rendering it almost impossible for any stranded vessel to escape destruction."[79]

In the afternoon of February 20, 1858, Thomas Jefferson Mulford (1801-1883), keeper of the Napeague Life Saving Station, while on horseback and headed to the Ditch Plain Life Saving Station, discovered wreckage and a seaman's chest on the beach. Word spread and by nightfall, bodies were being found along the coast, "encased in great blocks of ice, some singly, others clasped together, frozen in with timbers and oars and a thousand and one other objects which are spumed forth from a dying ship—what Walt Whitman called 'the shatter of the sea.' "[80]

The site of the wreck, five miles west of the Montauk Lighthouse, about where Shadmoor State Park is currently located, was a scene of chaos. The ship had apparently crashed into the rocks and was totally destroyed. There were 33 on board, only about two-thirds of which were recovered; their identities unknown to eastern Long Islanders.

The funeral was held at the Presbyterian Church at East Hampton. In his sermon the Rev. Stephen Mershon mournfully reflected upon the lost souls:

It is not the member of our community, whose name has often sounded in our ears; it is not the long known friend; it is not the relative, not the dear member of our domestic circle, that we have come to bury. No! We have come to bury the stranger. No father, no mother, no wife, no sister, attends this burial, to moisten the grave's cold earth with their tears…

With feelings of due solemnity, then, let us give a Christian burial to these shipwrecked mariners, who have been cast upon our shores…

A LEGACY OF VALOR

It was but the deed of a moment. Masts, spars, sails, officers and crew, were all in one confused mass! O, what an awful moment! How intense must have been the agony of the surviving! Their early terror was soon taken away. Their agony in time was but momentary, for sudden destruction came upon them.[81]

Site of John Milton shipwreck, currently at
Shadmoor State Park in Montauk, 2008
(Author photo)

They were buried in the Old South End Burying Ground in East Hampton. The ship's captain, Ephraim Harding, and his son Rodolphus were interred in Tisbury on Martha's Vineyard.

The *John Milton* faded into history for nearly seventy years until Long Island historian William Donaldson Halsey (1860-1939) presented a reasonable theory as to the cause of the wreck in 1927:

This was before the days of ocean telegraph, and there was no way of communicating with a distant port, except by other vessels, and this was very uncertain...A vessel was sailed according to the latest charts published at the time of sailing, and on a voyage of many months duration, perhaps around the globe, many a change might be made in these charts of which the navigating officers of a ship might be entirely ignorant. And there was no way by which they could get this knowledge...

When the John Milton left the Atlantic seaboard, Montauk Light was a steady light, and was the only light out of Fire Island. Ponquogue Lighthouse was built in 1857, and was first lighted on January 1, 1858, and was made a steady light, just as Montauk had here-to-fore been, and Montauk was changed at that date to a flash-light.

Now, it is entirely probable that Captain Harding did not know of the new light house at Ponquogue, nor of the change from steady to flash light at Montauk. This being the case, and presuming, which is entirely possible, that Captain Harding, in a lull in the storm, had sighted a steady light, thinking of course it was Montauk, steered his ship accordingly, and if this were the fact, his course would have taken him directly into Block Island Sound, just where he wanted to go.[82]

In 1890, Dr. Abel Huntington (1850-1907), son of coroner Dr. George Huntington (1811-1881), a young lad at the time of the wreck, recalled memories of when he accompanied his father to view the grizzly scene of dead bodies:

It was a sad, sad sight that our eyes were called to witness as all those stark and frozen bodies were brought and laid side by side in ghastly rows awaiting, some, the recognition of friends who came to claim them, but most, for the rite of simple sepulture at the hands of kind strangers in that quiet village by the sea.

I can close my eyes now even at this remote time, and vividly recall the whole weird sight; and no lapse of years can efface the deep and lasting impressions then made on my boyish fancy...

All vestiges of the wreck have long since vanished from sight and to day no one standing upon that memorable spot and looking out over the quiet, slumbering sea, would for a moment think that it was at one time the theatre where occurred so terrible a tragedy.[83]

Regardless of the cause, the wreck of the *John Milton* remains a significant part of Montauk history, and the monument at the Old South End Burying Ground is a silent reminder to those who were lost on that fateful day nearly 160 years ago.

The John Milton Monument in the Old South End Burying Ground, East Hampton, marks the spot where many of the bodies were interred. Photo taken 2008. (Author photo)

The ship's bell from the John Milton is shown at the Montauk Point Lighthouse Museum, February 2016. (Author photo)

NOTABLE SHIPWRECKS 1600S – 1877

A. L. Hardy (1858)

On May 4, 1858, the schooner *A. L. Hardy*, carrying 2,500 bushels of corn, went ashore about 13 miles west of the Montauk Lighthouse. It was believed that the ship's captain mistook the newly operational Shinnecock Lighthouse at Hampton Bays for the Montauk Light. In addition to the captain, the crew contained his two brothers and a young teenager. As soon as the ship struck, one of his brothers was washed overboard. The captain and his other brother endeavored to reach shore but they too were swept away in rough seas. It was two days later when the young boy was rescued. The cargo was salvaged.

The grounding took place about five miles west from the location where the *John Milton* had met its fate only three months earlier.

Emma (1862)

The schooner *Emma*, of St. Andrews, New Brunswick, sailing from Matanzas with a cargo of molasses and bound for Portland, Maine, came ashore in a snowstorm five miles west of Montauk Lighthouse on February 3, 1862. All aboard were safe. The keeper at the Ditch Plain Life Saving Station, George Lester, "threw a line by means of the mortar and thus saved the crew."[84]

Great Eastern (1862)

The incident involving the *Great Eastern* left a permanent mark at Montauk Point. Though it was neither a shipwreck nor a grounding, its story has a special place in Montauk's maritime history.

At the time of its construction in London in 1858 it was the largest ship in the world (692 feet long, 120 feet wide, with 6 masts and 5 funnels). Designed by naval architect Isambard Kingdom Brunel (1806-1859) for use in transporting emigrants to America from England, the iron steamship carried passengers for several years.

On one of its voyages from England to New York in August 1862 the *Great Eastern* had 1,530 passengers and a large amount of freight which increased its draught to 30 feet. Under these conditions the captain decided to avoid entering New York Harbor over the bar at Sandy Hook and instead sail around Montauk Point, traverse Long Island Sound, and dock at Flushing Bay.

During the clear, calm, early morning hours of August 27 the great ship was within sight of the Montauk Point Lighthouse. Two miles to the northwest of its position was the Endeavor Shoals, a dangerous hazard only 19 feet below the water. It fell to the ship's pilot to safely navigate the channel between it and the Point. While in progress, about a mile and a half east of Montauk Point, a rumble was felt aboard ship, apparently the result of running against a rock. An inspection revealed no leakage and the ship continued on toward New York, listing to port as it sailed.

A LEGACY OF VALOR

Great Eastern
Billed as the largest ship in the world when built in 1858, the
Great Eastern is shown in 1865, carrying the trans-Atlantic cable.
Its name lives on in the waters off Montauk Point when the
ship was damaged by a rock in August 1862.

A model of the Great Eastern dominates the other displays in the shipwreck room of the Richard T. Gilmartin Galleries at the Montauk Point Lighthouse Museum. Photo taken February 2016. (Author photo)

Once at New York, and after all passengers were safely put ashore, it was discovered that the rock had opened an 83-foot-long, 9-foot-wide gash. Thanks to double-hull construction (almost three feet between each layer), the ship did not sink, saving many lives.

The story did not make the pages of *The New York Times* for nearly a month, when a description of the repair work was reported. In December, when the work was completed, *The Times* reported the presentation of the following certificate to the Agents of the Great Eastern Company:

> *We, the undersigned, having carefully examined the steamer Great Eastern, and the repairs, which have been done in a scientific and workmanlike manner, are of opinion that she is in every way seaworthy and in a condition to carry passengers with safety and comfort,*

and a full cargo of any description, to any part of the world. The accident and subsequent occurrences have fully demonstrated the great value and safety of a double bottom.[85]

The *Great Eastern* continued as a passenger steamer only until 1864 when it was converted for use as a cable-laying vessel, successfully laying the first lasting trans-Atlantic cable in 1866. The once mighty ship gradually faded into obscurity, being converted for use as a floating music hall by 1878 and finally as advertising for Lewis's Department Store in Liverpool. It was finally broken up for scrap between May 1889 and November 1890; ironically the only time in its history that it made a profit.

The Salt Lake Herald offered a postmortem for its contribution to history:

If there is a shade of regret that such a noble ship has been sent in pieces to the junk shop, it is also relieved by the fact that even the failures of this largest ship of the world are honorably connected with the subsequent triumps [sic] of naval architecture.[86]

The rock struck by the *Great Eastern* off Montauk Point has long since been noted on navigation charts. Jeannette Edwards Rattray quoted from a statement made following the inspection of the ship after it struck the rock:

Later, soundings made off Montauk revealed the presence of a rock needle, theretofore unknown, that reached to within twenty-four feet of the surface. For whatever consolation Captain Paton might derive from the fact, the Great Eastern had made a contribution to American hydrography. The needle was named the Great Eastern Rock, and still bears that name on mariner's charts.[87]

The great poet Walt Whitman (1819-1891) wrote of the mighty ship:

Nor forget I to sing of the wonder,
the ship as she swam up my bay,
Well-shaped and stately the Great Eastern swam up my bay,
she was 600 feet long,
Her moving swiftly surrounded by myriads of small craft
I forgot not to sing.[88]

In February 2013 a model of the *Great Eastern* was exhibited for the first time at the Montauk Point Lighthouse Museum. The eight-foot-long model, on a scale of 1:95, is a lasting reminder of Brunel's "Great Babe."

Merganser (1865)

In early February 1865, while three smacks from New London were in the process of towing the brig *Merganser*, a snowstorm severed the lines. The crew aboard the *Merganser* anchored the vessel and left. Next morning it was discovered sunk in 20 feet of water two miles offshore. The ship's owners planned to raise it.

Amsterdam (1867)

On October 21, 1867 the British steamer *Amsterdam*, of Leeds, England, Captain Gibson, sailing from Malaga to New York, came ashore opposite Third House in a dense fog. The cargo consisted of grapes, raisins, lemons, Malaga wine, and Spanish lead. As reported in the Sag Harbor *Corrector*, "She lies on the rocks and is partly filled with water. It is doubtful whether she can be got off."[89]

Almost a year later, October 1, 1868, the wreck and the cargo of lead were sold at auction for $646; the vessel for $221 and the lead for $425.

In 1970 a diver recovered the nameplate which indicated that the ship was only a year old when it met its end.

The section of beach where the ship grounded has forever been known as Amsterdam Beach. Land in the area was set aside to become Amsterdam State Park in 2005, featuring hiking trails.

William Faxson (1868)

The schooner *William Faxson*, went ashore twice at Montauk within a week. Sailing from Boston to Philadelphia with a cargo of glue material, it went ashore one mile west of the Montauk Lighthouse on February 26, 1868. A wrecking company from New York came out and refloated the ship on March 3 at a cost of $2,700. While being towed in heavy seas, it sprang a leak.

The ten men aboard stayed with the ship as long as possible, until a heavy snowstorm forced them to man a lifeboat, "and after beating about nearly all night in a freezing storm landed near one of the Government Boat Houses [Ditch Plain Life Saving Station]. The schooner went ashore again about opposite Stratton's [Third House]. Her stern is gone and cargo scattered."[90]

The wreckage and beach-strewn cargo were sold at auction about a week later for $80.

Mary Milnes (1869)

An unusual cause for a shipwreck on Long Island took place on September 8, 1869, when a tornado struck and wrecked the schooner *Mary Milnes* on Montauk. The captain, Frank C. Parker, lost his second mate (his brother David Parker), who was thrown from the mast and killed. Another crew member, P. E. Delliver, was also lost. Both bodies were later found on the beach. Delliver was buried on Montauk.

The ship's remains were sold at auction for $670 on September 14.

This severe storm on eastern Long Island caused much damage, including the destruction of the barn on the grounds of the Montauk Point Lighthouse. A new barn was built on the site in 2015.

Jennie Lee (1871)

The schooner *Jennie Lee*, "sumptuously equipped," with nine persons aboard, caught fire and burned to the water's edge about nine miles off Montauk Point shortly after midnight on October 2, 1871, with the loss of two people. Aboard were the ship's owner, O. B. Jerrolds, a wealthy landowner from Denver, Colorado, his wife and three children, a servant, and three crewmen.

An account of the tragedy was recorded by *The Brooklyn Daily Eagle*:

Shortly after midnight Mr. Jerrolds had occasion to go on deck. Springing out of his berth, somewhat confused with sleep, he was going toward the stairs when a sudden lurch of the vessel, caused by abrupt tacking, pitched him against the centre table. As he fell, his outstretched hands clinched the lamp chains which were hanging from the ceiling. The lamp was dashed to the floor, and in a very short time the vessel was enveloped in flames. Mr. and Mrs. Jerrolds made the most frantic efforts to save the life of their child [Jennie, age 4]. They were, however, with difficulty got into the small boat and their lives saved…

A reward is offered for the recovery of the bodies, and efforts to that end are being made, but the task seems hopeless.[91]

Loss of Three Fishermen; "The Mystery of Montauk Point" (1873)

Though not a shipwreck, the loss of three fishermen at Montauk is an intriguing chapter in Montauk's maritime history. The journal of the Ditch Plain Life Saving Station normally recorded daily weather conditions and passing ships, but on December 19 events were recorded as follows:

A boat from the next Station West No. 5 [Napeague] went off in the fore part of the day with a crew of three men belonging to the Station Albert Edwards Albert Halsey Alexander Osborn to try for cod fish, they was last seen from the Station about Eleven o clock am on the fishing ground, it soon after began to thicken up & rain about 4 pm the Boat was found drove ashore 3 miles west of the Station supposed to have been capsized off shore and the crew lost, the oars & mast belonging to the Boat were found in diferent place along the beach[92]

The Journal for the next day simply noted, "… went off in the fore part of the day but could see nothing of the missing Boats crew."[93] No additional notations were made.

The Journal for the Hither Plain Station for December 21, 1873 indicates another search was conducted: "Launch boat and look for bodies of missing men find none."[94]

The three men — Albert Edwards, 45, of Amagansett, George Alexander Osborn, 19, of Montauk, and Albert Halsey, 23, of Bridgehampton — were known to be good swimmers.

The date of their demise is given as December 19. "The cause will in all probability remain a mystery, as there was no surf, or high wind, and all were good boatmen."[95]

A funeral service was held at the Presbyterian Church at East Hampton on December 22.

As late as July 1876 it was said that "speculation is active, but unrevealing concerning the fate that befell them…the event will never be other than it now is —— "The Mystery of Montauk Point."[96]

Albert Edwards's name is among those engraved on the Lost at Sea Memorial at the Montauk Point Lighthouse.

Montrose (1876)

On December 16, 1876, the ship *Montrose*, bound from Gibraltar to New York, went aground at Montauk in a severe storm. The "sea was running very high, and when she struck on the bar, the surf made a clean beach over her, washing away all the deck houses." Attempts to run a line to the stranded vessel proved ineffective. To make matters worse, the ship had already encountered five days of stormy weather and the crew "were so exhausted as to be almost helpless when she struck."[97] After being constantly battered by the angry seas, the ship broke up. At least three crew members were lost.

Circassian (1876)

One of the most disastrous shipwrecks that occurred off the shores of eastern Long Island was that of the British ship *Circassian*. The full-rigged iron vessel, 280 feet long, carrying general cargo, first ran on the sandbar opposite Bridgehampton, during a snowstorm late in the evening of December 11, 1876. All forty-nine aboard were safely rescued through the efforts of the surfmen from the Mecox Life Saving Station. Then the Coast Wrecking Company was hired to salvage the cargo. Among the 32-man crew assigned to the task were 10 Shinnecock Indians, who stayed aboard ship during the operation.

After more than two weeks of work, a storm developed on December 29 and quickly intensified. Convinced that the *Circassian* would dislodge itself from the bar with the next high tide, the captain refused assistance to abandon ship. The snow and winds intensified and high seas pushed in, pounding the vessel and causing panic aboard. A distress signal was sent out.

The signal was seen by the patrol from the Mecox Station, but attempts to land a line on board or launch a surfboat by station captain Baldwin Cook and his crew were futile, and by midnight the ship was being pounded to pieces. In the *Annual Report of the Operations of the United States Life-Saving Service for the Fiscal Year Ending June 30, 1877,* it was noted that, "In the tremendous sea then hurling thousands of tons of water each moment upon the beach, no life-boat, even if unbroken by the weight of the surf, could have been propelled from shore."[98] Men seen on deck were pitched into the turbulent waters. Of the 32 on board, 28 were lost, including the ship's captain, John Lewis, and all of the Shinnecock Indians. One of the survivors died shortly after.

Jeannette Edwards Rattray described the sorrowful plight of the Shinnecocks: "The doomed Indians could be heard at intervals above the howling wind and roar of the waves, singing hymns and praying as they hung in the rigging. Now and then the moon came through the clouds, and they could be seen."[99]

Although the wreck took place about 30 miles west of Montauk, the tragedy touched the shores of Montauk, when several bodies were swept eastward with the current and washed ashore in the vicinity of the Ditch Plain Life Saving Station over the next few weeks, as reported in the journal kept by the station:

> *Tuesday, January 2- Found since Sunday six more bodies.*
> *Wednesday, January 3- One more body found this morning.*
> *Tuesday, January 9- Found 4 more bodies on the beach today.*
> *Tuesday, February 13- Found to day one mile west of station, the body of a man, probably one of the Circassian's crew.*
> *Wednesday, February 14- An inquest was held to day over the body found yesterday. The body was identified as that of Thos Or, carpenter's mate, of the ship Circassian.*
> *Monday, February 26- Found another body to day one mile west of the station probably one of the Circassian's victims, making 27 found, and but one remaining.*
> *Tuesday, February 27- An inquest was held to day over the body found yesterday, which was that of an Indian.*[100]

◀ A LEGACY OF VALOR

The bodies of the 10 Indians were interred in the cemetery on the Shinnecock Indian Reservation just west of Southampton. Eleven seamen were buried in the Old South End Burying Ground in East Hampton. Other burials were at Southampton and Brooklyn.

The wreck of the Circassian at Bridgehampton in 1876 caused a number of bodies to be washed ashore on Montauk beaches.
(Montauk Library)

The four survivors of the Circassian disaster are depicted in this engraving, thoroughly exhausted on the beach near Bridgehampton in December 1876. (Frank Leslie's Illustrated Newspaper, January 20, 1877)

Idalia (1877)

On August 31, 1877, the British brig *Idalia*, of Georgetown, Prince Edward Island, sailing from Bonnaire in the Caribbean for Providence with a cargo of salt, came ashore about two miles west of the Montauk Lighthouse after having sprung a leak. The crew was housed at the Ditch Plain Life Saving Station and later taken to Sag Harbor where they boarded a ship for New York. The ship was a total loss, but was sold, since "some of the sails are new, and the standing rigging good, but the hulk is in bad condition."[101]

CHAPTER 7

Notable Shipwrecks 1878 – 1914
The U.S. Life Saving Service Years

WITH THE CREATION of the United States Life Saving Service in 1878, there were more stations along the shores of Long Island and elsewhere to respond to maritime incidents. During its existence, crews from the Ditch Plain and Hither Plain stations at Montauk responded to a number of ships in distress along Montauk's shores.

Hattie V. Kelsey (1878)

The schooner *Hattie V. Kelsey*, of New Haven, bound from Georgetown, D.C., to New London with a cargo of coal, ran aground on the bar in thick fog near the Ditch Plain Life Saving Station on August 2, 1878. The entire crew was removed safely by members of the Ditch Plain and Napeague Life Saving Stations. After the cargo was removed, the vessel was refloated and able to continue on its journey.

After being rescued, the ship's captain, H. M Randall, wrote of the actions taken by the crew of the Napeague Station: "I cannot speak of the [lifesaving] service as a whole, but I do know, if the crew of No. 7, Dist. No. 3, are a sample of the Life Saving Service which girts our coast, then are the lives and property of seafarers in safe hands … our experience with those we met while on the beach was pleasant, and will long be remembered."[102]

John D. Buckalew (1882)

On February 18, 1882 the schooner *John D. Buckalew*, of Perth Amboy, New Jersey, bound for Newport, Rhode Island, carrying 180 tons of coal was wrecked at Gin Beach, on Montauk's North Shore. The wreck occurred shortly after 1 a.m. in the midst of gale-force winds. Unfortunately for the men on board, the location of the ship "was beyond the scope of the service, far from any habitation, the nearest life-saving station being some miles distant, on the other side of the island, on the ocean shore, with the high land of Montauk intervening."[103]

Capt. Patrick Gough lowered the lifeboat to get ashore as soon as possible but his two crewmen refused to go because they could not swim. Once ashore, soaked and freezing, the captain wandered aimlessly about in the darkness, searching for help. At daybreak he came upon Second House, where he told his story to proprietor George Osborne and others. He was conducted to the Hither Plain Life Saving Station where he received care.

A LEGACY OF VALOR

The lifesaving crew started out for the site in the hope of saving the ship's crewmen. They arrived only to find the ship broken apart, the pieces strewn along the beach as far as could be seen. There was no sign of the two crewmen. Men from the Ditch Plain Station joined the search. Hours later, the bodies of the two men, Thomas Green and Lester Cohen, were found on the beach about a mile and half west of the wreckage by members of the Hither Plain Station. They were buried in the Old South End Burying Ground in East Hampton, near the site of members of the *Circassian* shipwreck of 1876.

Captain Gough remained at the Hither Plain Station for three days until he was able to travel to his home in New Jersey.

Lucy Morgan (1883)

On November 16, 1883, the *Lucy Morgan*, a 16-ton schooner from Saybrook, Connecticut, bound for Fort Pond Bay, lost its cables and went ashore at Fort Pond Bay in a strong northwest gale. The crew of three and party of five fishermen were saved by the crew from the Hither Plain Life Saving Station. Since the vessel was only 16 tons, the captain's only request was for lines to refloat his vessel, which was accomplished in a timely manner.

Lizzie M. Dean (1886)

On February 10, 1886, the three-masted schooner *Lizzie M. Dean*, of New York, wrecked at Shagwong Reef at Montauk Point during a storm. The ship was headed from Baltimore to Providence with 1,100 tons of coal. Due to poor weather conditions the ship's crew remained with the vessel until February 13, when the crew of eight made their way in fog to Third House. The proprietor, Theodore Conklin, notified keeper Frank Stratton of the Ditch Plain Life Saving Station, who took six of the men to the station and cared for them for two days. Clothing was provided for them by the Women's National Relief Association. The station crew went to the vessel to prevent it from being washed away. However, the ship proved to be a total wreck, with only the sails and rigging being salvaged. The captain and his mate remained with Conklin at Third House. About a week after the incident, a wrecking steamer from New York came and took charge, stripping the vessel of anything worth salvaging.

NOTABLE SHIPWRECKS 1878 – 1914

Keeper James Scott is shown seated on the front porch of the dwelling at the Montauk Point Lighthouse. Scott undoubtedly witnessed a number of vessels that came ashore in the vicinity during his 25 years at the Lighthouse (1885-1910).
(Brooklyn Daily Eagle)

The Lewis King is shown aground not far from the Ditch Plain Life Saving Station. All aboard were safe and the cargo of dates appeared on dinner tables for months.
(Montauk Point Lighthouse Museum)

Lewis A. King (1887)

The 150-ton schooner *Lewis A. King* of Ellsworth, Maine, bound from New York for Boston with a cargo of clay and dates valued at $1,000, went aground at 12:30 a.m. on December 19, 1887. It came ashore almost head-on in a storm about a mile and a half west of Montauk Point. The ship's captain, H. C. Farnham, had lost his bearings and mistook the Montauk Lighthouse for the Watch Hill Lighthouse at Rhode Island. The five crewmen and the captain's sister came ashore without incident.

Capt. James G. Scott (1885-1910), keeper of the Montauk Lighthouse, did not notice the vessel until a crew member appeared at the station. In addition, the Ditch Plain Life Saving Station crew did not know because the location was beyond the range of their jurisdiction. It seemed that the sailors thought there was a manned lifesaving station near the Lighthouse and attempted to make contact with it. However, the signals were hidden by the ship's sails and could therefore not be seen. In addition, the vessel had run ashore near high bluffs, which made it difficult to distinguish.

Captain Scott took in the entire group at the Lighthouse. Later, three crewmen went to the Ditch Plain Station and were tended to for eight days.

It was thought that the vessel could be refloated without difficulty. Captain Farnham telegraphed the Scott Wrecking Company of New London for assistance. However, subsequent efforts to refloat the ship proved fruitless and by November 1890 the *Lewis A. King* was abandoned.

The cargo of dates provided servings of date pudding in East End towns for months.

Favorite (1888)

Early reports painted a portrait of another Montauk mystery surrounding the 17-ton fishing smack *Favorite*, of New London. While on a fishing trip, it lost its mast and sprang a leak in a storm several miles off Montauk Point on August 22, 1888. It grounded about four miles west of the Montauk Lighthouse and very near the Ditch Plain Life Saving Station. The station captain, Frank Stratton, was the first to discover the ship. No one was aboard when it came ashore, and it was feared that the crew had drowned. A few days later it was discovered that the crew had been safely removed by the revenue cutter *U. S. Grant* and taken to New London. According to the ship's captain, Dunbar, "… the *Favorite* was caught in the gale and her mast carried away, receiving other damages that caused her to commence filling until she was in a sinking condition, and we were forced to take to the yawl in which we remained until rescued."[104]

Not realizing the ship's crew had already been removed, keeper Stratton hastily assembled a crew of surfmen (who were on vacation at that time of year) and set up a watch. He also removed all valuable commodities from the vessel and secured them.

Although there were plans to haul off the old vessel (built 1832), by the end of September, the *Favorite* was going to pieces and any hope of refloating it were abandoned.

George Appold (1889)

The steamer *George Appold*, guided by Capt. William Fields, 1,456 tons burden, bound from Providence to Newport News, Virginia, ran aground in clear weather and high tide around 1:30 a.m. about a mile and a half west of the Montauk Lighthouse on January 9, 1889.

By 10 a.m. the following morning, the weather looked threatening and the keeper ordered his men ashore, since a distance of half a mile had to be negotiated over rocks. Captain Fields declined to leave the vessel with his crew, but had the passenger sent ashore. As the weather worsened, the Ditch Plain Life Saving Station summoned assistance from the Hither Plain Station. Together they assembled the apparatus, launched the breeches buoy, and safely unloaded the ship's 27 crewmen. By the time the last man had been safely taken ashore, waves were sweeping over the ship. Six crewmen were cared for at the Ditch Plain Station for two days, dry clothing provided by the Women's National Relief Association.

Blame for the grounding was placed on the second officer, who was on duty at the time, and apparently disregarded the orders from the captain as to what course to follow. It was alleged by the crew at Ditch Plain that this officer

> was the same man whom the same life saving station man 'warned' off the same rocks two years ago and the same boat also. Had the same man at the wheel kept on turning and had he room enough, it is apparent to all that the vessel would have turned completely round and returned most likely to Providence. It was most extraordinary steering."[105]

It was thought that the ship could be refloated without difficulty, but it was learned that instead of remaining on the outer bar, the storm that followed raised it up and forced it on the rocks, ripping a hole through the bottom. About two weeks later the ship reportedly had broken up.

The cargo, as described by Jeannette Edwards Rattray, consisted of "one hundred barrels of New England rum, a great quantity of calico in ugly colors, some rather coarse clothing, and heavy, cheap shoes." There were dozens of wagons that came from neighboring communities to see what might be salvaged along the beach. Wrote Rattray:

> *Thrifty mothers wore house dresses, aprons, and sunbonnets for years, made from a certain chocolate-brown calico with white rings on it, or another pattern in red and yellow, and made it into little girls' school dresses…*
>
> *There was a great time matching up the shoes. Children hated to wear them, because their copper toes marked them as "wreck shoes." Bits of the calico are still in evidence; it went into patchwork quilts when the dresses wore out.*[106]

The Suffolk County News in 1959 described the wild scene:

> *…men, women and children joined in the "treasure hunt," coming with horses and farmwagons from miles away, some wagons becoming so overloaded with booty and passengers that they mired near the beach and had to be unloaded before they could be extricated.*
>
> *Declared one county weekly: "This was the most disgraceful exhibition of illegal greed in eastern Suffolk County's long history of free-for-all salvaging."*[107]

The good intentions of people in salvaging portions of the cargo were marred by individuals with other motives. Reportedly:

> *Several parties obtained a whole wagon-load of shoes, boots, stockings, hats and underwear, enough to last them their natural lifetime. Small boys stowed bundles of stockings, etc., under their coats. Isaac Conklin's house on Montauk was broken into, and goods stored there by the wrecking company were stolen. The Coast Wrecking Company's agent, Mr. Pierson, will try to compel people to return the goods.*[108]

Although there were comments made about the children not being able to afford regular shoes, and the calico was sometimes referred to as being "ugly," there were no complaints regarding the recovery of the barrels of rum!

The total value of the ship was $75,000 and the cargo $70,000. Since the ship was a total loss, the estimated savings of the cargo amounted to $12,000. Items were auctioned off by the wrecking company. According to former East Hampton Town Historian Sherrill Foster (1921-2007), the list of items included "166 pieces of bleached muslin, 14 pieces of unbleached muslin, 34 pieces of mull dress goods, 275 pieces of calico and ginghams, 150 pieces of alpaca, 2 cadies of Ladies hose, 328 empty oil barrels. Well, so much for the barrels of New England Rum!"[109]

Taking an excursion by water is highly unusual in winter months around Long Island, but about a week after the initial grounding, a party of approximately 50 came to view the wreck; and since the ocean was so calm they were able to come within about 100 feet!

NOTABLE SHIPWRECKS 1878 – 1914

Example of Engineer's log for the George Appold from a voyage in October 1888. The steamer ran aground at Montauk Lighthouse on January 9, 1889. The ship is remembered for its cargo of copper-tipped "wreck shoes." (Montauk Point Lighthouse Museum)

Joseph (1892)

On October 16, 1892, the *Joseph*, a 1,542-ton ship, of Nova Scotia, sailing from New York to London with a cargo of 9,800 barrels of petroleum and 1,000 cases of gasoline, valued at $50,000, went ashore at Shagwong Reef, two and half miles west of the Montauk Lighthouse. Crewmen from the Ditch Plain Life Saving Station took the crew to safety. The Scott Wrecking Company of New London successfully hauled it off, enabling the vessel to proceed to London.

Elsie Fay (1893)

A severe snowstorm on the night of February 17, 1893, caused the three-masted, 172-ton schooner *Elsie Fay* to be driven ashore about two miles west of the Montauk Lighthouse at about 9:30 p.m. Sailing from Grand Cayman, West Indies, for Boston, carrying logwood and coconuts valued at $6,000, Capt. F. P. Miller and a crew of six were rescued by the crew of the Ditch Plain Life Saving Station, who launched two lifelines. The rescued men were cared for at the station for six days. Assistance in the operation was provided from Hither Plain station crewmen.

A visit to the wreck the next day determined that it was quickly going to pieces and the cargo would be considered a total loss — except for the coconuts.

According to Jeannette Edwards Rattray, "Montauk people had coconuts in every style for about a year, and were sure to be given coconut cake whenever they were invited to a company meal in Amagansett or East Hampton."[110] The *Sag Harbor Express* advised: "Merchants, take warning, they [the coconuts] will be cheap for a while."[111]

There was no blame with the grounding since, during the heavy storm the:

> Captain could neither see Montauk Point light or hear the fog horn, thinking he was making deep water and east of Block Island. The tide was strong west. This made the miscalculations, as it was much stronger than the wind, and when the vessel struck, thought they were on Block Island. The surf was running strong and high, but notwithstanding this the crew were made comfortable in the forecastle, until about fifteen minutes before the life savers succeeded in reaching the schooner with the life-line, when they were safely landed within a short time.
>
> Much credit is due the Captain and crew of the [Ditch Plain] station for their skill and the manner in which they performed their duty, and for their hospitable treatment and care of the wrecked crew.[112]

Nearly all of the crew's possessions were lost. One casualty did occur, however — that of the ship's parrot, "which was the Captain's room mate, and the crew's advisor." When the ship grounded, the bird became "all excitement, and talked of their danger constantly, and the last time it was heard, remarked to the crew that they were in hell now; 'good-bye.' The parrot froze, the crew mourn its loss."[113]

An interesting note is that one of the ship's masts was purchased by Frank Sherman Benson of Montauk, who had it moved there.

The area where the ship wrecked has since been known as "Coconuts."

Fannie J. Bartlett (1894)

A unique reminder of a shipwreck found its way onto the timetable of the Long Island Railroad for many years. The three-masted, 831-ton schooner *Fannie J. Bartlett*, bound from Philadelphia to Boston, carrying 10,000 tons of coal valued at $3,500, became a total wreck on the beach about two miles west of the Hither Plain Life Saving Station in rough weather and heavy fog at 4:30 a.m. on January 16, 1894. The captain, A. T. Hutchins, lost his bearings while following a pilot boat, which also ran ashore east of Amagansett.

An anchor was run out to prevent the vessel from coming ashore and a tug was dispatched. With assistance from the crew of the Napeague Life Saving Station, the ship's 10 crewmen were brought ashore due to increasingly poor weather conditions.

By afternoon, when weather conditions improved, the ship's crew returned to the vessel in a failed attempt to refloat the schooner. At that point a tug arrived to take over the operation, so the lifesaving crew headed back to the station, only to be recalled when it was discovered that the tug had abandoned efforts to refloat the ship.

The ship's crew were again taken to the station. Attempts to refloat the ship over the next three days proved unsuccessful, the waves gradually pounding the ship to pieces. By January 23, anything that could be salvaged was taken ashore.

In February the wreck and cargo were purchased for $96.

At the time of the wreck the Long Island Rail Road reached as far east as Bridgehampton, about twenty miles short of its ultimate destination on the shores of Fort Pond Bay, Montauk, which extension was completed in December 1895. Along the new railroad, the "Bartlett" stop became a flag station that served as a convenience for fishermen at Napeague and for the crew of the Napeague Life Saving Station. According to Jeannette Edwards Rattray, the nameplate from the vessel was most likely posted at the stop by Nathaniel Dominy Sr. (1827-1910) of East Hampton, who maintained a fishing shack at Napeague for many years. The "station" closed down at the end of December 1928.

Oriole (1894)

The 250-ton schooner, *Oriole*, from New Bedford, bound from Providence for New York with a cargo of empty barrels valued at $300, grounded near Culloden Point at 9 a.m. on November 25, 1894. The ship was caught in stormy weather in Block Island Sound, causing the loss of its forward mast, resulting in the vessel drifting aimlessly into Fort Pond Bay. The crew came ashore in their own boat and were tended to at the Hither Plain Life Saving Station. In January 1895 the ship was sold at auction to Peter Koppelman of Springs for $26, with some of the spars from the ship used for a liberty pole at East Hampton.

Mary A (1896)

The *Mary A*, a seven-ton schooner, capsized and sank in a storm on June 16, 1896. Keeper William Parsons from the Hither Plain Station discovered its bowsprit sticking out of the water and, since it was off-season and there were no crewmen available, set out in a boat alone. With aid from volunteers and the ship's crew the vessel was taken to shoal water and the two men aboard were rescued. The ship was later raised and remarkably sustained only minor damage.

Ella May (1897)

The six-ton sloop *Ella May*, from Greenport, was dragged ashore in a heavy gale about a mile and a half north of the Hither Plain Life Saving Station on November 9, 1897. Next morning surfmen from the Hither Plain and Ditch Plain stations dug a channel, which, at high tide, enabled the ship's crew to refloat the vessel.

A V H (1897)

The eight-ton sloop *A V H* went aground in Fort Pond Bay during a storm on November 12, 1897. The ship's two crewmen found shelter in a nearby fish house, but were later taken to the Hither Plain Station until the weather improved. The combined efforts of members of the Hither Plain and Ditch Plain stations made repairs and the ship was refloated on November 16.

Shamrock (1898)

The two-masted schooner *Shamrock* was driven ashore in 60-mile-per-hour winds at Jones Reef on April 30, 1898. The three Connecticut fishermen aboard were safely landed. Montauk Lighthouse keeper James Scott described the storm as the worst he had experienced since coming to the Lighthouse in 1885. The ship was badly damaged.

Argus, Coastwise (1899)

The steam tug *Argus*, with the barge *Coastwise*, containing 1,000 tons of coal in tow, from Perth Amboy, New Jersey, to New London, went aground at Turtle Cove, just west of the Montauk Point Lighthouse on June 15, 1899. The *Argus* appeared to have lost the Lighthouse in dense fog and attempted to round Montauk Point too soon.

The coal was pumped overboard by the Scott Wrecking Company and within a few days both vessels were abandoned. The crews of both vessels (15 in all) were cared for by keeper James G. Scott at the Lighthouse.

Later that month, an expert diver reported both vessels as total wrecks.

In July, a man named William Slater received a contract to wreck the *Argus*, which sat in just twelve feet of water. He claimed he would need to use dynamite in order to retrieve the boiler and any other useful machinery on board.[114]

By late September it was reported that coal was seen frequently washing up on the beach, reaching some 200 to 300 tons' worth when the remains of the *Argus* were completely broken up by October.

Fannie (1902)

The nine-ton sloop, *Fannie*, lost its anchor cable in strong northwest winds and stranded about four miles west of the Montauk Lighthouse on October 29, 1902. Due to difficult weather conditions the lifesaving crew did not see the vessel until next morning. The combined efforts of members from the Ditch Plain and Hither Plain stations succeeded in removing the six men aboard. The sloop was hard aground and the decision was made by the owner to abandon it.

Exception (1903)

While sailing off Montauk Point in thick fog on the night of September 5, 1903, the *Exception*, a 417-ton, 2-masted British schooner, from Bonaire, West Indies, to Boston with a cargo of salt valued at $2,000, stranded about a quarter mile east of the Ditch Plain Life Saving Station. The captain had mistaken the Montauk Lighthouse for that at Gay Head, Martha's Vineyard; the "recent alteration of form to third class light [at Montauk] was unknown to Captain Baxter and caused his mistake." Next day, surfmen went out to the vessel to discover "she was resting easily and not leaking."[115] Two days later the owner was taken on board and soon after the schooner was refloated by tugs from the Merritt, Chapman Wrecking Company.

Cuba (1903)

On December 18, 1903, the 453-ton British barkentine *Cuba*, of Windsor, Nova Scotia, bound from New York to Port Grenville, Nova Scotia, stood in a precarious position about a mile off the north side of Montauk Point. Later, it went ashore at Oyster Cove. The crew of eight were safely removed and tended to for four days at the Ditch Plain Station, but the ship was a total loss. The fact that the night was clear and calm raised questions as to what could have caused the grounding, though the captain claimed he mistook the light at Montauk Point for that at Little Gull Island. Later, it was reported that the second mate was in charge at the time the boat came ashore.

On December 28 a survey was conducted and the vessel was condemned, "she having seven feet of water and sand in her hold, her keel gone and her planks stove." The vessel was sold at auction two days later.

Pendleton's Satisfaction (1905)

The three-masted schooner *Pendleton's Satisfaction*, sailing from St. Petersburg, Florida, to Providence with a cargo of lumber, ran short of provisions and anchored abreast of the Hither Plain Life Saving Station on March 9, 1905. The crew said that the trip from the Outer Banks of North Carolina to Montauk took 24 days and that they were "the roughest days they ever experienced on the water." The stormy weather destroyed the ship's sails, and the cargo had shifted, causing the boat to list. In addition, the men were constantly pumping water as the ship was leaking badly. Since the journey took longer than expected, the crew of nine men were found by the lifesavers to be "in bad shape. Captain Bunker reported that he was short of provisions, the only thing left on board to eat being one loaf of bread, and that the crew had been on short and constantly decreasing rations for eight days." The Hither Plain crew obtained $20 worth of provisions and took them to the starving crew.[116] Additional provisions were provided, enabling the ship to continue its journey to Providence.

Buena Ventura (1906)

The *Buena Ventura*, originally part of the Spanish Navy and captured by the United States in the Spanish-American War, was ultimately reduced to service as a coal barge. It was being towed by the tug *Walter A. Luckenback* on December 7, 1906, when, in a heavy northeast gale, it foundered a mile and a half east of Montauk Point with the loss of three crewmen.

A crewmember of the *Luckenback* singlehandedly rescued two men from the doomed vessel. The heroism of Mitchell Bruso was described by Jeannette Edwards Rattray:

> *Bruso rowed a small boat to the sinking barge and rescued Captain Ollie Owarsond, whom he found with his clothing frozen to the topmast. He rowed back and put the helpless captain onto the tug. Without a moment's hesitation, covered with ice from head to foot, he put out again and released a seaman, Charles Martin, who was frozen to a floating hatch. Bruso's shipmates looked on while the little boat looked likely at any second to be swamped by the towering seas.*[117]

On December 16 the remains of the *Buena Ventura* were blown to pieces by the revenue cutter *Mohawk*, to prevent it from being a menace to navigation. According to *The New York Tribune*:

> *The work of destroying the old barge was a difficult one, particularly as a heavy sea was rolling in so that the boats from the Mohawk could not get near the wreck. At last the cutter steamed within a hundred yards of the two masts sticking above the water and then a couple of barrels of oil were emptied through the scupper holes. The oil smoothed the seas, and two of the boats rowed over the wreck and sank four mines on her decks. The explosion blew out both masts and a greater portion of the decks, so that the Mohawk was able to steam over the wreck in seven fathoms of water.*[118]

Matanzas (1908)

An eerie sight accompanied the grounding of the 1,579-ton barge *Matanzas*, near the Hither Plain Life Saving Station on January 27, 1908. The *Matanzas*, of Fall River, Massachusetts, was bound from Philadelphia to Boston with a cargo of coal, valued at $7,920. It was being towed by the tug *Concord*, and, during a storm, the lines broke. The captain and crew were rescued by the Austrian steamship *San Giovani*.

Although there was no one aboard the ship when it hit the beach, a human leg was found, and it was thought to have been from a member of the ship's crew. Hither Plain Capt. Carl Hedges, remained on watch for bodies that might have come ashore.

The *Matanzas* soon broke up.

Winifred (1908)

On February 4, 1908, the *Winifred*, a 2,794-ton British steamship from Boston to Philadelphia, became disabled 12 miles southeast of the Montauk Lighthouse. Lighthouse keeper James Scott was notified by signals. Fifteen passengers were removed by members of the Ditch Plain Life Saving Station, "where they were thawed out at the station after their twelve-mile trip in the surfboat and then taken across the point to the railroad depot, bound for New York."[119]

The crew at the Ditch Plain Life Saving Station located the steamer drifting and flying distress signals, and for a time it appeared the ship was headed for the rocks. The lifesavers readied their equipment, but it was soon determined that the steamer had anchored and was secure. A boat from the ship came ashore to identify the vessel and explain that the thrust shaft had broken, causing the loss of its propeller.

Tugs came the next day and took the *Winifred* to New York for repairs.

Chippewa (1908)

A truly remarkable rescue at Ditch Plain took place on the night of June 23, 1908, when Capt. Barksdale Macbeth and a crew of 24 from the Clyde liner *Chippewa* were rescued off Montauk Point by a group of auto drivers who operated the breeches buoy at the Ditch Plain Life Saving Station. They accomplished the feat in the absence of the lifesavers, all of whom were on vacation. Capt. Carl H. Hedges was in charge of the station and was alone on duty when the ship stranded.

The *Chippewa*, 275 feet long, 40 feet wide, and 2,155 tons burden, bound from Charleston, South Carolina, to Boston with a cargo (valued at $150,000) of lumber, 39,000 watermelons, alligators, and ostriches (the animals were for a museum), ran aground on the rocks three miles west of Montauk Point on the night of June 23. It was thought that the vessel could be saved, and work was under way by the Merritt-Chapman Wrecking Company to remove the ship from the rocks.

When the ship grounded, several holes were broken through the ship's port side, bringing in cascades of seawater, knocking out the steam power. Consequently, no alarm whistle could be sent, and the crew had to wait until the fog lifted. When all was clear, Captain Macbeth came ashore in a boat to request aid.

Captain Hedges, alone at the Ditch Plain station, saw that the ship was close enough to be reached by breeches buoy, but without his crew available to help, nothing could be done. He contacted other stations for aid, with negative results. He resorted to asking some fishermen in the area, but they had no knowledge of how the Lyle gun apparatus functioned. However, sensing the anxiety of the moment, the fishermen climbed into wagons and ran off in search of aid.

The Clyde line Chippewa aground at Montauk, 1908. Since it was off-season, civilians aided in the dramatic rescue of all aboard. The vessel suffered damage but was eventually refloated. (Montauk Point Lighthouse Museum)

They met up with three cars about two and a half miles from Montauk Point. The situation was explained to the motorists. These "good Samaritans," Mr. and Mrs. William Post, Mr. and Mrs. Frederick Post, William Titus, and Mrs. Scott Libby, all of East Williston, Long Island; Mr. and Mrs. David L. Van Nosten and Miss Viola Van Nosten of Great Neck, Long Island, and Emmett Woodruff of Flushing, New York City, followed the fishermen back out to the Point.

The chauffeurs had sufficient mechanical knowledge to operate the gun. After three failed attempts, the fourth shot was secured aboard the ship. By the time the first man came ashore, darkness prevailed and the waves had become more intense. Though the waves swept over each man in the breeches buoy, all made it safely to shore, to the cheers of a crowd that had gathered. By 10 p.m., Captain Macbeth was the last to set foot on land.

The cargo, including the alligators and ostriches, was saved. The ship itself was a total loss.

An investigation into the actions taken by Captain Macbeth and second officer Clinton Googins aboard the *Chippewa* revealed that the ship would not have been stranded had proper soundings been taken to determine the ship's position. Both men pleaded guilty and had their licenses suspended for thirty days. As stated in *The Master Mate and Pilot* in June 1908:

> *This should be a lesson to navigators running on our coast at night or in thick weather. The Chippewa, like other steamships of her class, carried a sounding machine, but didn't use it for some reason. The Board of Supervising Inspectors made the rule requiring that machine, and the owners bought it to be used. The expense of using it is a mere trifle. The labor is little, and it does not delay the ship at all. The plain question is: What is the use in carrying such a machine if you don't use it?*[120]

In addition to the thousands of watermelons recovered from the *Chippewa*, an interesting find was an ostrich egg. It was not known if the egg washed ashore or was carried from the ship, but Ditch Plain keeper Carl Hedges treasured it for many years.

The East Hampton Star reported:

> *Almost every family within a hundred miles of Montauk has eaten watermelon from the wrecked steamer…Scores of motorboats…hovered around the steamer last week, offering and giving aid in the removal of the melons to the lighters and taking their liberal toll…The fruit was peddled from wagons in many Long Island and Connecticut villages.*

Attempts were made to save the vessel, including the dumping of cargo. Consequently, numerous motorboats began hovering around the *Chippewa*:

> *to reap the harvest of watermelons which are being jettisoned to lighten the vessel preparatory to an effort to save her. The Chippewa's crew welcome the motor boats, as those aboard willingly volunteer assistance on the steamer in return for the gift of melons which are so easily obtained. Many thousands of the melons have already been gathered by the motor boats, with the big flow of fruit still showing no signs of abating. Owing to the fact that very few melons escape the vigilance of motor boats, very few reach the shore to reward the patience of the scores of beach-combers congregated there.*[121]

Large amounts of the lumber were cast overboard, which were also snatched up rapidly. The *Chippewa* was refloated on August 4 and towed to New York.

George M. Grant (1911)

The *George M. Grant*, 1,254-ton schooner, of New Haven, headed for Newport News, Virginia, with a crew of 10 and no cargo, went aground about 10 p.m. a mile north of the Montauk Lighthouse on February 24, 1911. Capt. Carl Hedges of the Ditch Plain Life Saving Station reported that because of the position of the ship, his crew could not reach it with their surfboat or rocket guns. Later in the day, the crew from the stranded vessel came ashore on one of the ship's boats. At the time of the grounding, the ship was in the charge of the first mate, who supposedly had lost his bearings. Two days later the *Grant* was hauled off and towed to New London for repairs as it was leaking badly.

Ontario (1912)

During the early morning hours of Monday, April 8, 1912, the Merchants and Miners 3,082-ton steamer *Ontario*, en route from Baltimore to Boston with 77 persons aboard and general cargo, grounded at Montauk, three miles east of the Ditch Plain Life Saving Station, as a fire raged in its hold. The cause of the blaze originated in the cargo, which consisted mainly of cotton, resin, turpentine, and whiskey. There were also shoes, peanuts, tobacco, oysters, kale, and canned vegetables aboard.

Once the fire became threatening, Capt. William J. Bond ordered the wireless operator, Hubert Ingalls, 19, to send out an "S O S" signal. *The New York Times* noted his heroic efforts:

> *Ingalls...stood by his key flashing the signal "S O S," the wireless call for help, until the flames reached the wireless house, with the result that the intense heat to which the apparatus was subjected rendered it useless. The wireless room was black with smoke for fully fifteen minutes before Ingalls left it, but he stuck to his post as long as the instrument worked and even then protested against leaving, hoping against hope that something would happen to put his key in commission again....*
>
> *His little wireless hut on the deck was almost directly over the burning part of the ship, and life within it was almost unbearable. But that had no effect on Ingalls.*[122]

An hour later Captain Bond directed the ship for Montauk Point rather than risk the vessel being burned at sea. It should be noted that he, as well as Ingalls, acted heroically in the face of danger, as also reported by *The New York Times*:

> *...he and First Officer Harding remained at the wheel in the pilot house until the heat was so intense that they had to take the wheel at intervals of a few seconds, it being impossible for any man to hold it for more than a few moments at a time. They did not leave the house until the ship was beached, and when they staggered out were both nearly overcome by the dense smoke in which they had been compelled to work in order to beach the vessel.*[123]

When John E. Miller, keeper of the Montauk Point Lighthouse, was advised that the steamer was coming ashore, he "laughed at the report and declared he saw nothing to warrant such a belief. Ten minutes later the men at this [Ditch Plain] station saw the ship on the rocks, hurried off with a breeches buoy apparatus and later dragged their surfboat on its truck three miles over the beach to the burning steamer."[124]

Once it was evident that there was a dangerous situation aboard ship, the male passengers quickly dressed and assisted the crew in battling the fire. The women "were kept in the saloon and were not informed of the desperateness of the situation."[125]

With assistance from members of the Hither Plain and Watch Hill (Rhode Island) Life Saving stations, the crew at the Ditch Plain Station acted valiantly in the rescue of the 32 passengers, standing by to take off the ship's crew if necessary. None of the passengers were injured, but they were clearly shaken by the experience.

Carl Hedges, keeper at the Ditch Plain Station, wired New York to send wrecking tugs and revenue cutters to Montauk Point.

After spending nearly two days battling the blaze and increasingly rough seas, Captain Bond and his crew abandoned ship, being transferred to the revenue cutter *Acushnet* and the tug *Tasco*, which pulled up nearly. All were taken to New London. The timing was perfect, as shortly after the transfer of all aboard, an explosion blew off the steamer's deck, leaving only the ship's hull.

The fire created quite a spectacle. As reported by *The New York Times*,

> *Great clouds of jet black smoke poured up from the ship, while every few seconds long tongues of fire would leap high into the air, following the explosion of turpentine barrels. So terrific was the heat in the ship that the iron plates on the…sides became red hot and the glare from them could easily be distinguished from the shore.*[126]

Considering the nature of the cargo, especially the large quantity of cotton, it was expected that the fire would burn itself out after about a week.

One member of the lifesaving crew at Ditch Plain, David Miller, suffered a severe injury. While setting up the breeches buoy an axe head flew off its handle and hit him in the head, causing a fractured skull. He was transported to St. Mary's Hospital in Jamaica, New York, in critical condition. His condition rapidly improved as he was able to return home about a week later.

Word came initially to keeper Walter H. Davis of the Watch Hill Life Saving Station that the *Ontario* was on fire and would have to be beached at either Montauk Point or Block Island. Davis and four crew members set out in rough seas in search of the steamer. Unable to find it, they spotted rockets in the air a distance west of Montauk Point, indicating that the ship was probably in the vicinity of the Ditch Plain station. Soon the *Ontario* came into view, beached on the Montauk shore.

Keeper Davis wrote of the events that followed:

> *Ours was the first boat of any description to reach the disabled steamer. The life-savers from Ditch Plain had, however, arrived on the beach abreast of her somewhat ahead of us and rigged up the breeches buoy apparatus. Running our boat in alongside and going aboard, we discovered that the whipline operating the buoy had snarled, and that the buoy itself was hung up 100 feet or more from the port forerigging, to which the hawser supporting the buoy had been made fast. I at once climbing into the rigging, overhauled the ship, cut out the knot,*

spliced the line with the aid of two of the ship's crew, and then signaled for those on shore to haul away. The buoy was thereupon run out to the steamer. The distance between the vessel and the shore was about 700 feet, and the operations from the shore were conducted from the crest of a bank 80 feet or more high.

After the tide had made ebb and the seas somewhat abated, Capt. Parsons of the Hither Plain Station, arrived with his power surfboat towing an open surfboat, and all hands began the work of transferring the passengers and their baggage to the wrecking tug Tasco. I and my crew carried the first load, consisting of 12 women, in one of the Ontario's boats. Capt. Parsons and his crew also transferred a load in his surfboat, and the ship's second officer concluded the work of transfer in another of the steamer's boats, the 32 passengers and their baggage being taken off by 9:30 a.m.

While the transfer of passengers and their effects was going on the Ditch Plain life-saving crew came aboard in the breeches buoy and joined the vessel's crew in fighting the fire…At the request of the captain of the Ontario we remained on the vessel overnight and assisting in fighting the fire. At 5 a.m. of the 9th, there being nothing further we could do, and all hands being greatly exhausted, we returned to our stations.[127]

The *Acushnet* stood by until the early morning of April 10. Then it sent a wireless message:

Anchored 5 A.M. off Ontario. Wind moderate, northeast breeze with a long southwest swell. When direction of wind changed flames went aft. Deck all burned away and vessel aflame fore and aft. We picked up two missing men and ship's boats. Have them on board. Could not recover hose and lines. No further assistance needed, as nothing can be done. We leave for New Bedford. Consider it useless for you to come out here.[128]

The combined value of the *Ontario* and its cargo was $630,000, of which $395,000 was lost.

In appreciation for the "invaluable service to the passengers and crew" of the *Ontario*, Captain Carl Hedges of the Ditch Plain station and his wife went on a two-week vacation to Baltimore as guests of the Merchant and Miners Line, owners of the stricken steamship.

On April 30, what remained of the *Ontario* was hauled off by the Scott Wrecking Company and taken to Promised Land at Napeague for preliminary repairs. This was accomplished with some difficulty, as seas were rough and the ship was leaking badly. Approximately $25,000 worth of cargo was still aboard, consisting mostly of tobacco and whiskey. About two weeks later the ship was towed to New London for rebuilding.

The site of the disaster at Montauk was within a few hundred feet of the *George Appold*, which wrecked there in 1889.

According to Bradley Sheard in his book, *Lost Voyages; Two Centuries of Shipwrecks in the Approaches to New York*, the cooperative efforts of the two revenue cutters with the crews of the Ditch Plain and Hither Plain Life Saving Stations in the *Ontario* incident:

...caught the attention of Congress, who had been searching for ways to cut the federal budget. On January 28, 1915, the Revenue Cutter Service and the Life Saving Service were officially merged into one service, to be called the United States Coast Guard. This new service had the combined assets and strengths of its two parent organizations, consisting of 45 cutters, 280 life-saving stations and 4,155 personnel.[129]

George Curtis (1912)

The menhaden fishing steamer *George Curtis*, out of Greenport, grounded about two miles southwest of the Montauk Lighthouse in dense fog on June 4, 1912, and became a total wreck. Capt. Charles Baldwin claimed the ship's compass was malfunctioning at the time of the incident. Capt. Carl Hedges at the Ditch Plain Life Saving Station saw the ship go aground while on patrol. Since it was near summertime, there was no crew at the station, so Hedges summoned his wife, his son Wilson, and a visitor, Mrs. Dickinson, to assist. Together, they positioned the breeches buoy apparatus and prepared to launch a line to the stranded vessel. However, through the fog, they spotted a second fishing vessel (name unknown), which pulled up and removed the 15 crew members of the *George Curtis* without incident. They were taken to Promised Land, Napeague.

The ship, owned by the Atlantic Oil and Fertilizer Company at Promised Land and containing about 400 barrels of fish, was raised about two weeks later and taken to New London for repairs.

CHAPTER 8

Notable Shipwrecks 1915 – 2000s
The U.S. Coast Guard Years

THE CREATION OF the United States Coast Guard on January 28, 1915, brought an end to the old Life Saving Service, which had performed its duties magnificently during the past 37 years. Many of the practices established under the leadership of Sumner Kimball were maintained by the new organization. With an increase in local fishing and pleasure boating, the Coast Guard, aided by new developments in technology, maintained a high level of respectability in responding to ships and boats in distress during the 20th century and beyond.

Thomas R. Woolley (1921)

The *Thomas R. Woolley*, a two-masted schooner, grounded on a sandbar south of the Montauk Lighthouse on November 28, 1921, after drifting dismasted for two days following a storm. The crew signaled the Montauk Lighthouse and were spotted by assistant keeper Jack Miller. Attempts to launch a breeches buoy and a surfboat were fruitless due to wind conditions. Finally, the crew of seven boarded a dory in an attempt to reach the shore, but it soon capsized in rough seas, and they washed up on a sandbar only 300 feet from shore. At this point, Coast Guard men, under Capt. Joseph Clark, formed a human chain at low tide to get the seven-member crew safely to the beach.

Madonna V (1922)

The Montauk Peninsula was a lively place during the Prohibition era when numbers of liquor-laden "mother ships" would lie at anchor in waters beyond U.S. jurisdiction in what was labeled "Rum Row" and await the arrival of small boats to transfer the precious cargo ashore. One such craft was the schooner *Madonna V*, of Halifax, Nova Scotia. Referred to as a "rakish craft which … possessed unusual speed," the *Madonna V* was sailing from Nassau, Bahamas, and bound for St. Pierre, in the Gulf of Lawrence. Reports varied as to the number of cases of whiskey aboard; ranging from several hundred to as many as 3,000, valued at $100 a case!

On December 21, 1922, in a heavy gale, the ship grounded at Napeague. Crewmen from the Napeague Coast Guard Station attempted rescue using a power surfboat, but the seas were too rough. A breeches buoy was launched, and the eight-man crew of the stricken ship were safely rescued.

There was no worry about securing the cargo, as it reportedly was being "salvaged by willing hands."

Wrote Jeannette Edwards Rattray, "Lifelong teetotalers and even deacons of the church risked pneumonia in the Montauk surf to bring it ashore, prompted no doubt by the inherited custom of 'wrecking' and old New England principles against waste of any kind."[130]

Hundreds of visitors descended upon Napeague to view the wreck, "and it has made many of them feel thirsty to realize that there were hundreds of cases of refreshments of the choicest variety likely to be lost." Local fishermen recovered several cases that were floating by. Others standing on shore "regretted that they were not equipped with hip boots so they could wade out and grab a case or two."[131]

Fantastic stories resulted from the grounding:

> *One man arrived at the scene of the wreck early enough to see fifty or more cases of liquor floating to the west, just far enough off shore to make it impossible to land them....*
>
> *...those who managed to land a case or two are reported to have at least a dozen hidden away. One man told a story that he had twelve cases of Scotch in his garage, and the door was unlocked. He had placed a stick of dynamite on each case for protection...*
>
> *It is reported that several of the local boys are going to build a bridge from the shore to the wreck and see what is in her hold.*
>
> *Other local wreckers are forming plans to use a sand sucker under the boat and pull the "stuff" from her hold with hooks. It is reported that the stock in this company jumped fifty points when this idea was disclosed.*[132]

Osprey (1929)

The 409-ton beam trawler *Osprey*, bound for New London after a fishing trip at Georges Banks (a large fishing area between Cape Cod and Cape Sable Island, Nova Scotia), ran aground in dense fog three miles west of the Montauk Point Lighthouse on September 7, 1929. Though situated about 600 feet offshore, the ship was not leaking and its cargo of 80,000 pounds of halibut was secure.

Captain Frank Warner and his crew at the Ditch Plain Coast Guard Station set up the breeches buoy and removed several of the 22 crew members, while the rest came off in their own boats.

Although beaching at a spot where there are numerous rocks, the *Osprey* managed to find a sandy spot. The vessel was refloated the next day by two Coast Guard cutters and a sister ship, the *Penguin*. There was no damage to the *Osprey* and it proceeded to its destination, the Groton, Connecticut, plant of the Atlantic Coast Fisheries Corporation.

A local Montauk resident, Harold Hone (1882-1939), provided assistance to the Coast Guard who was:

> *...kind enough to aid the men by the use of his sedan in hauling the beach equipment over rough roads to the scene of the accident in less than an hour, whereas it would have taken several hours at best otherwise. He also stood by the men, and at daybreak on Sunday, he was on hand with containers of hot coffee for all hands. Mr. Hone lives near the Ditch Plain Station.*[133]

Harry Bowen, Petrel, and Tattler (1930)

A dense fog on the night of November 17, 1930, caused difficulties for three vessels in the vicinity of Montauk. The 3,522-ton freighter *Harry Bowen*, carrying 5,000 tons of coal, bound from Norfolk, Virginia, to New Bedford, went on the rocks at Ditch Plain. Although Coast Guard cutters were unable to get near the ship due to rough surf, a breeches buoy line was shot aboard.

Aid came from Coast Guard stations at Hither Plain, Napeague, Amagansett, and Georgica (East Hampton).

Finally, "the grim determination of 35 gaunt and red-eyed men not to give up their ship through the long weary hours when it seemed that only a miracle could prevent its breaking up on the jagged rocks off Montauk Point were rewarded this afternoon"[134] when, as seas became calm, they were all removed via the breeches buoy by the crew of the Ditch Plain Coast Guard Station, who toiled for hours in rain, fog and wind.

The ship's crew had begun tossing parts of the cargo overboard in an attempt to lighten the vessel, hoping it would enable the ship to be easily hauled off the reef. Six days after it grounded, the *Harry Bowen* was successfully hauled off the reef and made it safely to New York City.

Since the grounded ship was easily seen from shore, numerous onlookers gathered to view the rescue operations, some offering assistance. Even photographers and filmmakers traveled to Montauk to witness the activities.

Meanwhile, 23 fishermen were rescued in surfboats by the Ditch Plain crew from the trawler, *Petrel*, which had run on the rocks off Block Island in fog described by seasoned sea captains as one of the thickest in years. The vessel was inbound from Georges Banks to New London.

The situation aboard the *Petrel* was dire. The grounding caused the engine room and boiler room to flood, and the men "clung for hours to the rigging with icy seas dashing over them, and nine of the fishermen were at the point of exhaustion."[135]

Once the crew of the ship was safely removed the vessel was left to the mercy of the sea.

A third vessel, the fishing steamer *Tattler*, responding to the S O S from the *Harry Bowen*, also grounded. All aboard were safely removed by Coast Guard personnel from New London.

Comanche (1931)

On January 4, 1931, the fishing boat *Comanche* came ashore below the Montauk Lighthouse. Margaret Buckridge Bock, daughter of lighthouse keeper Thomas Buckridge, recalled years later, "Fortunately, no lives were lost. We made coffee and sandwiches for them, and some of them came into the house to 'dry out,' since they were all slightly inebriated."[136]

Algie (1931)

The Canadian power boat *Algie* was forced to ground just northwest of Montauk Point in the morning of February 15, 1931. Everett King, boatswain's mate at the Hither Plain Coast Guard Station, placed eleven men under arrest as they came ashore. Although the men admitted there was liquor aboard (3,550 cases), they "stoutly maintained their innocence of rumrunning and claimed that they were forced to run ashore when their craft sprang a bad leak."[137] The liquor was not removed from the vessel.

That night, Frank D. Warner, officer in charge of the Ditch Plain Coast Guard Station, took the 11 men to New York for questioning, where it was determined that the boat was bound from St. Pierre to Bermuda.

It was said that when the men were arrested, "there were about 20 men standing around the shore and it is the opinion of the local Coast Guard that the *Algie* fully intended to unload its cargo there."[138]

The day after the *Algie* came ashore, it was refloated by the Coast Guard and taken to New London.

Mavis (1934)

Superstition was supposedly to blame for the grounding of the 72-foot yacht *Mavis* on June 29, 1934. Its owner, Henry Burmeister of New York, intended to embark on a pleasure cruise around Long Island. Aboard were his daughter, Marian, and Miss Ottilie Hussman. A friend of Burmeister, Arthur Egeman, acted as crewman, and Erich Muehler was the captain.

They had departed from the Hudson River, off Riverside Drive, New York, four days earlier, and sailed through New York Harbor into the Atlantic, heading toward Montauk, where they would circle the Point and return via Long Island Sound, planning to dock at City Island, the Bronx. However, it ran ashore in dense fog at Montauk four days later, about a mile east of the Ditch Plain Coast Guard Station.

Egeman claimed he wasn't superstitious, but felt it was bad luck to have women on a ship. He relented when Mr. Burmeister said the two women "would do the cooking."[139]

Captain Muehler was more blunt:

> *Bad luck, women are. I ain't superstitious but I always seem to have bad luck when women gets around sailing ships. I don't know what the ole man's going to do with the two women, but I told him to ship them back to New York. I got my nose full of 'em....*
>
> *With them women on board we had nothing but calm weather and fog. The ole man said to bring the girls along for good company and they'd cook. I said I'd rather have an extra deckhand. The only time you should look at women on a boat is to look and see what they're getting into, or to stop them from getting walloped in the noodle with the boom.*[140]

All came ashore safely in a small dinghy. That evening the two women were driven back to New York, leaving the three men with the *Mavis*, which was towed to New London for repairs, since the hull had been damaged by rocks when it grounded.

Annie L. Wilcox (1934)

In what was described simply as "fishermen's bad luck," heavy seas and stormy weather spelled doom for the 1,250-foot fishing steamer *Annie L. Wilcox*, which grounded on Shagwong Reef around 1 a.m. on July 25, 1934. The steamer contained 300,000 pounds of menhaden and was on its way to the Smith Meal Company at Promised Land, Napeague.

It had been a foggy evening with some light rain. It was also low tide and Shagwong Reef, normally being eight feet below sea level, was only four feet below. Progressively rough seas made navigation difficult, causing the vessel to strike the reef. Capt. Edward Payne immediately gave the order to abandon ship. Moments after the crew of 20 were rowing ashore in six dories, the boat sank, but its upper portion remained visible above waterline. To make matters worse, a heavy thunderstorm struck as the crew came safely ashore.

Coast Guard cutters from Ditch Plain and New London raced to the scene, but by the time they arrived the crew of the *Wilcox* were already a safe distance from the wreck. All reached shore safely, but the cargo was lost, the fish seen floating over large areas of the bay between Montauk Point and Block Island.

The reason for the accident was stated as follows:

> *The mishap occurred when the captain of the boat ... gave over the wheel to one of his crew so that he could sleep for about an hour. Captain Payne laid out the course which was to be followed, but the man at the wheel shaved in a little to [sic] close and ran afoul of the shoal.*[141]

The *Wilcox* was later raised and towed to Greenport by the Merritt, Scott, Chapman Wrecking Company, where the vessel's engines were salvaged and the hull discarded. Built in 1872, it was said that "the new motors vibrated enough to open the old seams in the boat."[142]

Two views of the Comanche II beached adjacent to fishing pier directly below Montauk Point Lighthouse, 1935 (Margaret Buckridge Bock- Montauk Point Lighthouse Museum)

Comanche II (1935)

The reaction of the passengers to the grounding of the *Comanche II* on June 28, 1935, was that of experiencing a lighthearted episode. The boat came ashore just below the Montauk Lighthouse. Had not the weather been calm throughout, the craft would almost certainly have been smashed to pieces, since it ran on the rocks in a dangerous location.

The 50 passengers, many of whom were salesmen from the Underwood, Elliott, Fisher Company, were staying at the Montauk Manor. When it came time to leave the vessel, they:

> ...in an orderly and unceremonious way, donned life preservers and plunged into the roaring seas to find themselves in only four feet of water. The experience was something of a lark to the excursionists, but a real matter of fact disaster to Captain Joseph Morivec, who saw his $19,000 investment placed at the mercy of the sea and waves at one of the most exposed positions on the Atlantic Coast line.[143]

Apparently, Captain Morivec had misjudged the fog signal at the Lighthouse and allowed the ship to drift too close to the rocks at Montauk Point.

With the aid of Coast Guard and Montauk fishermen, the 55-foot vessel was hauled off three days later and taken to Montauk for repairs.

Raritan Sun (1935)

The 189-foot oil tanker *Raritan Sun*, sailing from Weehawken, New Jersey, to Phillipsdale, Rhode Island, carrying 165,000 gallons of petroleum, ran aground in dense fog about three miles west of the Montauk Lighthouse on July 14, 1935. The Coast Guard cutter *Perseus* responded and attempted to haul off the ship but the line between them snapped. Heavy seas prevailed during the early evening of July 15 and the ship's crew was taken off via breeches buoy by crewmen from the Ditch Plain Coast Guard Station.

The effectiveness of the equipment at the Montauk Lighthouse came into question as a result of this incident. After the ship grounded, Lighthouse keeper Thomas Buckridge wrote in his log:

> She grounded at about 4:30 pm in thick fog which came with southerly wind. Second Assistant [George] Warrington on watch. He had the fog signal going about 4:10 pm, as soon as we could see any indication of fog from here. The tanker hails from Philadelphia. There is considerable complaint that the sirens cannot be heard to the southwest where there is a wind at all from that direction.[144]

Superintendent of Lighthouses J. T. Yates wrote to the commissioner of Lighthouses in this regard: "The horns ... are not properly placed so as to give best results to the greater part of the traffic approaching this light station, for the greater part of the traffic approaches from a northerly or southerly direction."[145]

There were concerns from fishermen at Montauk about reports of oil leaking from the tanker and coming ashore as far west as Westhampton Beach, thereby ruining the fishing season. Even the Village of East Hampton and the Town Board began efforts to stop the possible dumping of oil overboard to save the ship without transferring it into another tanker. However, word came from the Ditch Plain Coast Guard

Station that no oil was observed ashore west of the grounded vessel. Perry B. Duryea said, "The reports are absolutely untrue, and it is the publicity that has done far more harm than any oil. The oil has practically all washed to the eastward and no harm has been done to the bathing beaches."[146]

Arthur Howe, secretary of the Montauk Yacht Club, made an aerial trip between Montauk and Westhampton to inspect the reported damage. He reported, "I saw no indication of oil and all the beaches were crowded ... The only oil that escaped the tanker was on Tuesday when a rough sea grounded the vessel on the rocks. Practically all of it floated around the point."[147]

Although the Coast Guard abandoned any hope of salvage, the Merritt, Chapman, Scott Company was hired to refloat the vessel as soon as weather conditions permitted.

Meanwhile, word of the incident began drawing crowds, as described by *The East Hampton Star*:

There is only a one track road leading from the polo field into the estate of Richard N. L. Church, which turns off to the beach and so to the site of the wreck. On Monday, hundreds of cars went on through to the Church property and left their cars there. After frantic efforts, the yard was finally cleared of cars and the remaining traffic went down to the beach to the east side of the Church property.

Five or 10 cars would attempt to leave on the return trip and would meet a like number of cars attempting to get in. after much arguing and horn blowing, one line of traffic would pull into the brush alongside the road to allow the opposing traffic to proceed. Some cars took an hour to get a half mile distance along the road.[148]

The *Raritan Sun* was refloated on July 20 and taken into Fort Pond Bay for temporary repairs, before being sent on to Boston for more permanent attention. According to *The New York Herald Tribune*, the thousands of gallons of oil had been lost, "to the vexation of fishermen and bathers up and down the coast ... The wind shifted to the east tonight and that means, fishermen say, that the oil film which was carried out to sea will be driven back to the Long Island beaches."[149]

Four days later, *The East Hampton Star* attempted to allay fears of oil contaminating Fort Pond Bay, as well as the Atlantic:

Visions of an oil slick over the entire bay grew into nightmare proportions. However, these fears proved to be unfounded for no oil has been reported. The damage to the shore on the ocean front seems to have been over-estimated. One good blow will probably clear the bulk of it away. At any rate, the constant menace to the fishing...has been removed...Large catches of fish are being taken every day by the excursion boats.[150]

Amelia D (1935)

The 20-ton fishing schooner *Amelia D*, swordfishing offshore and having a cargo of fish aboard, had anchored off Culloden Point. However, the anchor line chafed on rock, causing the ship to drift ashore overnight without warning on August 23, 1935.

The Coast Guard cutter *Algonquin* was easily able to refloat the vessel, but in the process the ship's keel was ripped off, causing it to sink immediately about 700 feet offshore. The six crewmen were safely removed by the cutter and taken to Newport, the lost ship's home port.

On September 1, the Merritt, Chapman, Scott Wrecking Company raised the vessel and transported it into Fort Pond Bay. Considered "a sorry sight as she emerged from her watery grave," enough water was pumped out so it could be transported to New London for repairs.[151]

Julia (1935)

The *Julia*, an 80-foot trawler, bound from New Bedford to the Fulton Fish Market in New York with 40,000 pounds of haddock, came ashore in dense fog a short distance west of the Montauk Lighthouse on November 13, 1935. The crew of four came off without incident.

In order to refloat the vessel, the cargo of haddock was first dumped into the ocean. In addition, since the ship was leaking badly, the Coast Guard sent for a pump to remove the water and fix the leak.

Mary P Mosquito (1936)

The 85-foot fishing schooner *Mary P Mosquito*, returning to Brooklyn from a long fishing trip with a crew of 13 (and a dog), grounded on the rocks in thick fog and rough seas about a mile west of the Montauk Lighthouse on November 26, 1936.

Since the boat began filling rapidly with water the order was quickly given to abandon ship. However, because of the poor conditions, the crew floated about in six dories as it was unsafe to risk landing. It took several hours until they were sighted by the Ditch Plain Station. Station Boatswain's Mate Earl M. Pike and a patrol set out in a motor boat. Since the weather was still unfavorable (over 30-mile-per-hour winds and fog), the Coast Guard crew simply drifted with the fishermen until conditions improved. Then they took the men aboard and took seven of them to the station, and the remaining six in their dories to Lake Montauk, where they were treated for exposure, and sent to New York by train next morning.

The *Mary P Mosquito* was completely demolished by the pounding waves.

Edna (1938)

The beam trawler *Edna*, capsized about seven miles southwest of Montauk Point on July 5, 1938. The boat's poor construction contributed to the mishap as it suddenly

> turned turtle and threw two of the three men into the sea from their high perches in the rigging where they had been looking for a fin. The boat had been previously rigged with a crow's nest aloft, a pulpit and other gear for swordfishing, and apparently did not have sufficient ballast.[152]

The three men managed to climb to safety on the keel. Ironically, as the Coast Guard surfboat was towing the craft to the safety of Lake Montauk, the boat righted itself!

Hurricane of September 21, 1938 (Tacoma, Ruth R, Ocean View)

A great number of vessels of all kinds in many areas were damaged or destroyed during the great hurricane which roared across Long Island in the afternoon of September 21, 1938. Packing high winds (gusting to 150 miles per hour at the Montauk Point Lighthouse) and incredibly high surf, houses, vehicles, trees, as well as watercraft suffered the cruel effects of what became the hurricane by which all others affecting Long Island would be measured.

At Montauk the beam trawler *Tacoma* was wrecked at Fort Pond Bay and not discovered until the end of November, about a half-mile off the gas buoy at Shagwong Reef. It was discovered in the netting of a trawler that was fishing in the area. A salvage crew dragged it into Fort Pond Bay where it was beached, surprisingly in good condition except for the rigging that was torn off in the hurricane. However, its captain, Seth Scribner of East Hampton, was not found. His name is inscribed in the Lost at Sea Memorial, located on the grounds of the Montauk Point Lighthouse.

The experience of the sloop *Ruth R* was terrifying for the men on board. On the day of the hurricane, the boat was off Culloden Point working on a fish trap. As weather conditions began to deteriorate, its owner, Capt. Dan Parsons, signaled for the men working in a separate "trap boat" to come aboard. However, one of the small boats, containing Cleveland Noel, capsized in the strong winds. It took some time for Wilfred Fougere and Joseph Guyetch in the other small boat to get to him and get back to the *Ruth R*. The wind completely destroyed the surviving boat leaving only the *Ruth R* afloat.

By then the storm was intensifying, and under full power, the ship attempted to reach safety, but the ferocity of the hurricane's winds drove the sloop over to Gardiner's Island, where they managed to anchor. Then the wind shifted, snapping the anchor cables. Parsons was unable to restart the *Ruth R* and, "the men were drifting with the full force of the hurricane in a general direction of Block Island. Not leaking, but taking aboard hundreds of gallons of rain water, the crew were pumping continuously all night to keep afloat."[153]

The *Ruth R* and its crew survived the storm, but on December 5, 1945, while work was being done on the engine, the engine exploded, blowing the roof off the newly-built pilot house. Although the cabin burned, the hull and deck were intact. Henry Bradford, who was working on the engine when it exploded, suffered burns and was taken to Southampton Hospital.

The *Ruth R* still had many more years at sea. Finally, on December 23, 1969, it was towed out to sea, 10 miles southeast of Montauk Point, and ceremoniously sunk.

Tragedy struck the bunker steamer *Ocean View*. Owned by the Smith Meal Company of Promised Land, at Napeague, the ship was headed there with 125,000 fish on board when the hurricane's fury caused it to founder quickly in Long Island Sound. Six of the 22 men aboard were lost.

The ship had gotten close enough to where the crew could see Plum Gut near Orient Point, Long Island, and there were hopes of beaching the vessel on the shore. However, with the engine disabled, the *Ocean View* drifted helplessly about in Long Island Sound. The 16 men who survived managed to get into one of the seine boats and came ashore near Madison, Connecticut.[154]

The names of 12 people who were lost in the hurricane are engraved on the Lost at Sea Memorial at the Montauk Point Lighthouse.

Princess (1945)

The fishing trawler *Princess* ran ashore at Montauk Point in dense fog on April 10, 1945, ripping a hole in the hull below water line. However, the boat managed to sail into Montauk Harbor, where a motor pumper from the Montauk Fire Department pumped the water out of the vessel. The trawler arrived safely at Greenport, its home port.

Sand Bay (1945)

An unusual rescue took place on September 2, 1945, involving the 38-foot fishing boat, *Sand Bay*, captained by Fred Schoendienst, with 15 men and 3 women aboard, which had been returning from a fishing trip when the boat's motor failed. One of the passengers, Ann Breyer, described what happened next:

> *Capt. Fred Schoendienst decided to let it drift toward a lighthouse, which was reached after two hours…We anchored close to the lighthouse, but no one saw us. The captain told us to pray for the anchor to hold. But at 3 A.M. it snapped and the captain told us we were at the mercy of the sea….*
>
> *At about 2 o'clock in the afternoon I thought I saw a ship about five miles away and told the captain. He said it was a buoy but soon I saw that it was a submarine [Navy sub Skipjack] rising out of the water. We yelled. The submarine saw us and blinked its lights. All of us just sat down and cried.*
>
> *The submarine came right alongside our boat and dropped lines so we could go aboard. It brought us to Montauk Point.*[155]

After safely delivering the fishing party the *Skipjack* continued to its base at New London.

Red Sail (1946)

The 40-foot dredger *Red Sail* piled on the rocks directly below the new seawall built around the Montauk Point Lighthouse on August 20, 1946. Encountering heavy seas as it rounded Montauk Point, "the forward deck was washed under, breaking off the swordfish pulpit which stove in the bow." As the ship began taking on water, the two men aboard, George and Richard Halliday, owners of the craft, elected to run the vessel aground and jump to shore.

The seawall was installed in 1946 as a preventive measure because of the severe erosion of the land surrounding the Lighthouse.

*Red Sail on rocks directly below Montauk Point Lighthouse, August 1946. The two men aboard jumped to safety on the beach.
(Montauk Library)*

Marpo V (1947)

It was quite a dramatic rescue that took place only a half-mile off Montauk Point on August 17, 1947, when the 42-foot party fishing boat *Marpo V*, of New London, sprang a leak in rough seas and foundered in just 10 minutes.

Two other Montauk party boats, the *Rex* and the *Ton-B*, happened to be nearby and raced to the scene, tossing life rings with lines attached to the vessel. The captain and all nine passengers were rescued, and just in time as Captain W. H. Libby was "already waist deep in the water. The others had already jumped into the sea and been pulled aboard the *Rex* and the *Ton-B*."[156]

All were taken to the fishing docks at the Long Island Rail Road in Fort Pond Bay and given dry clothing and hot drinks. The worst of their injuries was slight shock.

The *Marpo V* "had settled to the bottom in about 25 feet of water which left about 6 feet of her mast visible above the surface. Fishermen expressed doubts that the boat ... could be salvaged ... they surmised she would be broken up in a few days."[157]

Rose W (1949)

Two brothers, William and Felix Birch, from Mamaroneck, New York, were rescued when their 50-foot trawler, the *Rose W*, sprang a leak in the engine room and foundered about 20 miles south-southwest of Montauk Point on the morning of November 3, 1949. When the leak was discovered a pump was started but the vibrations from its operation opened the seam further, causing the vessel to sink.

The brothers set oily rags afire aboard the sinking boat to alert the Coast Guard plane that soon spotted the foundering vessel. They were able to maintain radio contact with the plane through a war surplus radio set until they had to abandon ship.

The two commercial fishermen, who had left Montauk Point for a three-day fishing trip, endured perilous high seas aboard a collapsible war surplus rubber raft for nearly an hour before being rescued by the crew of the fishing boat *Old Mystic*, of Stonington, Connecticut. They ended up in the safety of Montauk Harbor.

Both brothers were active in the Coast Guard during World War II, one at Montauk and the other on plane traffic duty at the Port of New York.

Pelican (1951)

What began as a holiday weekend excursion aboard the 45-foot fishing party boat *Pelican* ended as the worst maritime disaster in the history of Montauk. The vessel, captained by Edward Carroll, was equipped to handle only about 25 fishermen. But this was Labor Day weekend, and dozens of fishermen descended upon Fishangri-la at Fort Pond Bay to partake of the last opportunity for a good day's catch. A total of 64 people jammed aboard the *Pelican* for its ill-fated trip.

In spite of small-craft warnings, the *Pelican* set sail during the morning hours of September 1, 1951, settling in the "Frisbee Fishing Grounds," an area south of Montauk Point, to fish. While there, the weather turned ominous. Then one of the boat's two engines failed as Carroll attempted to take the boat back to the docks. Strong northeast winds were building and a light rain began to fall.

Many passengers became severely seasick, some going into the cabin in the hope of finding relief. As the seas grew rougher, the *Pelican* limped its way along on one engine. The ship's mate, Robert Scanlon, recalled the terrible scene which prevailed by 2:30 that afternoon:

> *One roller hit us and knocked us over, then another one, right behind it. It came over on top of us. It happened without warning...When the first one hit everybody rushed to the opposite side. Then another wave hit and over she went. A good percentage were down in the cabin due to the weather. They were trapped there when the boat turned bottom side up.*[158]

One of the divers sent down to retrieve bodies from the cabin said that the trapped fishermen "looked like they had been tearing each other to pieces" in a frenzied attempt to get out. Most bodies were found "piled up at the exit and the narrow passageway leading from the cabin." Said another diver, "It was just like a bunch of wrestlers locked together. I had to pry them apart to get in there."[159]

There were some other boats in the vicinity, making attempts to rescue the desperate fishermen. In the frantic moments that followed, there were some successes in saving them, but there were also those who, having clung to the floundering *Pelican* for a time, lost strength and slipped away under the water, never to be found. One of them was Captain Carroll.

Meanwhile, high atop the Montauk Lighthouse stood Archie Jones, officer-in-charge. He had been observing the *Pelican's* movements for some time. He had seen the storm building and the efforts made by other fishing boats to successfully return to port. Now it was the *Pelican* that remained.

Through binoculars, Jones could see that the boat was painfully overloaded and how, "with some desperation, people were clinging to the railing and struggling back up after getting knocked down. Through the rain he could barely make out Eddie Carroll on the bridge."[160]

Jones tried to contact Carroll on the radio but only received static in return. Then, when the *Pelican* had managed to sail north of the Lighthouse it seemingly could go no farther due to the force of the waves in The Rip.

Jones watched the events unfold for some time when he finally saw a huge wave strike and roll the boat over. Then there was a second wave, but "this time there was no rolling back. The boat kept going. Then Jones saw only the bottom of the hull."[161]

Frank Mundus's *Cricket II* and Carl Forsberg's *Viking V* began towing the *Pelican* into Montauk Harbor. Eventually Coast Guard vessels took over, taking the doomed boat into the harbor about 12 hours after the accident occurred.

A lifelong Montauk resident, Vincent Grimes, had been home on leave from his service in the Navy during the Korean War. He was one of those down at Montauk Harbor assisting in the recovery efforts after the *Pelican* was towed into the harbor. Upon discovering bodies still in the cabin he recalled,

> When we got enough water pumped out [of the hull] and we were down in the cabin, you could see where fingernails scratched in there, and you could see that these people evidently had an air pocket for a short period of time. They thought they could scratch right through, but hell, there was one-inch planking on the other side.[162]

The bodies were methodically taken onto the dock and moved to Perry Duryea's icehouse, which became a makeshift morgue. Since rigor mortis had set in the scene became even more macabre: "A foot stuck out here, a fist was raised there, a mouth frozen in mid-scream … It looked as though they had gone to sleep, then died in the midst of a nightmare."[163]

In the days ahead, the number of fatalities crept painfully higher as searches continued by sea and air. The final count was 45 dead, 19 saved, with a number of bodies unaccounted for.

An investigation was immediately begun by the Coast Guard. Capt. Howard Carroll, brother of the *Pelican's* lost skipper, broke down at the hearing, stating that the relationship between his brother and the fishermen was "not just a matter of hustling a dollar. These people are more than customers. They are what you might call friends. I know Eddie would have looked after his people."[164]

One man testified that it was not true that everyone rushed to one side of the boat when the waves hit, but did say that he "didn't hear the captain or the mate order the passengers to distribute themselves evenly about the deck." He believed the *Pelican* rolled over due to the high winds and waves.[165]

The blame was ultimately placed on Captain Carroll for allowing the boat to sail with too many people aboard, and, had he survived, he would have been charged with "gross and criminal negligence."[166]

As a result of the *Pelican* disaster, in 1956, President Dwight Eisenhower signed a bill requiring the Coast Guard to "inspect and certify any vessel that hired out for more than six passengers. At the time the

Pelican went down, the Coast Guard regulated boats of 15 tons and more, with no regard for the number of passengers."

John Behan, former state legislator and a Montauk resident, noted on the 50th anniversary of the disaster, "The *Pelican* is not something people out here want to remember. People still remember the bodies on the dock."[167]

When Robert Scanlon was questioned at the hearing as to the cause of the accident, he said, "The terrible, rough sea. The terrible, rough sea. That's what it was."[168]

Captain Carroll's name was engraved on the Lost at Sea Memorial at the Montauk Point Lighthouse. The *Pelican* itself, though still considered seaworthy, never sailed again.

Freda M (1953)

Perilous seas spelled doom for the 45-foot party fishing boat *Freda M* on October 11, 1953. The fishing excursion departed from Gosman's Dock at Lake Montauk early in the morning with Capt. George McTurck, of Sayville, Long Island, at the helm. As the boat sailed around Montauk Point the rough seas caused one of the fishermen to become so ill that the captain decided to take him ashore. Oddly enough, while sailing back, it spotted Captain Ole Olson's boat *Cigaret* in trouble, its engine having died. The *Freda M* towed it back safely. Then, although the seas were rough, the *Freda M* set sail again.

When they were about a mile south-southwest of the lighthouse, trolling near Jones Bar, tragedy struck: "One huge wave, which seemed to 'come up behind from no place,' to quote Captain McTurck, broke over the stern and pushed the bow almost vertically down into the water, twisted the boat over and split open the cabin."[169]

The six fishermen were washed into the turbulent seas, but since the vessel did not sink, they were able to cling to its side, although one of the men was missing. Another fishing boat, the *CMB*, was close enough to toss life jackets, preservers, and seat cushions, and picked up five fishermen.

A search for the missing fisherman involving some 30 fishing boats and 2 Coast Guard craft in the area turned up nothing.

The *Freda M* eventually was tossed ashore at Turtle Cove. Its condition was grimly described by *The East Hampton Star*:

> *The damage was extensive, her cabin had been ripped off, the roof dangled floating at her side. Several small holes in the underside spouted water and a portion of her stern was smashed on the rocks as she was buffeted in the waves coming in.*[170]

An investigation revealed that Captain McTurck's actions were appropriate and that there was no fault with the vessel or its equipment. McTurck's heroic efforts to save the missing fisherman failed since he was already holding up one man while attempting to throw life preservers to the lost fisherman. Recalling the recent *Pelican* disaster at Montauk in 1951, Chief Boatswain's Mate Purnell Curles of the Ditch Plain Coast Guard Station pointed out that there "were only a few passengers in the boat and there was no question of overloading."[171]

Mike Ahoy (1954)

While returning from a fishing trip out of Montauk, the fishing boat *Mike Ahoy*, with eight persons on board, blew up off Montauk Point, causing it to catch fire on July 29, 1954. It had been running at reduced speed because of heavy fog.

NOTABLE SHIPWRECKS 1915 – 2000S

There were actually two explosions. The resulting fire from the first was quickly extinguished but the second set the boat ablaze, causing injury to one fisherman. He was later taken to Meadowbrook Hospital [now Nassau County Medical Center] at East Meadow, Long Island. Another fisherman was blown off the boat by the explosion but was rescued with only minor injuries.

Fog delayed the Coast Guard in responding, but when Boatswain's Mate Purnell Curles, of the Ditch Plain Coast Guard Station, was able to throw a line to the burning boat, by then it had burned to the waterline and sunk.

All aboard were rescued by Captain George Hewitt's boat *Christopher*.

Unnamed Vessel (1955)

On June 1, 1955, a small pleasure craft chartered by five fishermen capsized in rough seas and ran aground at the foot of the Montauk Lighthouse. One man was lost, his body not recovered. Significant was the fact that the fishermen were not informed of the location of the life preservers. This incident was given attention by the Coast Guard because of the circumstances.

Photograph of the wreck of a motorboat at the foot of the Montauk Lighthouse as reported by the Coast Guard on June 1, 1955.
(U.S. Coast Guard)

Ripple (1955)

Four men were fishing near Shagwong Buoy aboard the 32-foot cabin cruiser *Ripple* on July 10, 1955. When they started the boat's engine, it exploded, resulting in a fire. The explosion was apparently the result of a leak in the fuel line, causing gasoline to seep into the bilge.

One of the four men, Henry S. De Plante, the ship's owner, suffered the worst of the situation. He was standing directly above the engine's hatch, and when the explosion occurred, he was blown overboard. He clung to the burning vessel until just before it went down. He and the others were picked up by two boats, the *4-Nix*, and the *Osprey*, both from Connecticut. De Plante was pronounced dead on arrival at the Coast Guard dock in Montauk Harbor, presumably of a heart attack, though he had also been badly burned.

Right after the men were rescued, a second explosion ripped the stern apart, and the *Ripple* burned to the water line and sank. Its home port was at Mystic, Connecticut.

The three survivors were taken by Montauk community ambulance to Southampton Hospital.

Scamp (1957)

The 16-foot outboard motor boat *Scamp*, noted for having logged about 12,000 miles in the previous five years, had been docked at the Montauk Yacht Club. While there it caught fire, apparently the result of a tossed cigarette, on August 14, 1957.

Thanks to one man's actions, a major catastrophe was averted:

> *An unidentified cab driver noticed the burning Scamp while making a late delivery, and with the help of several yachtsmen pulled the blazing outboard away from other craft. The cabbie's quick action is believed to have averted a possible wholesale holocaust since a fuel pump was only a boat's length away.*[172]

A spokesman for the Montauk Yacht Club concurred:

> *His quick action probably saved the entire yacht club. He said that if it had continued to burn unnoticed, the fire might have spread to a gas refueling tank. Everything, boats, clubhouse and docks, would have gone up then.*[173]

The boat's owner was asleep at the yacht club at the time of the fire and did not know what had happened until he spotted it on shore next morning. The boat was a total loss, but its new 35-horsepower Evinrude motor was recovered.

Undine (1959)

The 36-foot trawler *Undine*, under Capt. Richard Halliday, departed from Gosman's Dock in the early morning hours of May 3, 1959, and had been trawling about a mile and a half offshore, opposite downtown Montauk. Then trouble occurred.

When Captain Halliday tried to lift the trawl, the clutch on the winch jammed. The weight of the net put a heavy list on the boat, and one of the portholes went under and flooded. Capt. Halliday was on the bow when the boat sank under him.[174]

The trawler went down directly opposite Second House in downtown Montauk. Fortunately, the fishing boat *Netop*, operated by Richard de Waal, was nearby and quickly picked up Captain Halliday.

Captain Halliday might have harkened back to another time he had lost a boat. The dredger *Red Sail* ran aground on the rocks directly below the Montauk Point Lighthouse in 1946.

U.S.S. Baldwin (1961)

An unusual sight appeared on the beach just west of the Montauk Lighthouse during the afternoon of April 16, 1961. The decommissioned, 1,700-ton destroyer U.S.S. *Baldwin* was being towed from Boston to Philadelphia when the tow line from the tugboat snapped in rough seas about 23 miles south of Montauk Point.

The *Baldwin* was named for Civil War sailor and Medal of Honor recipient Charles H. Baldwin (1839-1911). Launched on June 14, 1942, it participated in the famous World War II invasion of Normandy on June 6, 1944, as well as other theaters of battle.

Within hours of being stranded off Montauk the huge unmanned vessel drifted to Turtle Cove, less than 200 yards from the Lighthouse and by next day grounded only 50 yards from the beach, in an area between Caswell's and Coconuts, resulting in the rupture of oil tanks on board and the appearance of an oil slick in the area.

Although the *Baldwin* was reportedly taking on water, there was no danger of its sinking or capsizing, since it was settled in only five feet of water.

Efforts were soon under way to haul off the ship. By April 26, the Navy had "thrown five salvage vessels, divers, and several hundred men into an effort to save the destroyer." Salvage operations were hard, a crew of 50 Navy men "heaving and hauling" aboard the *Baldwin*. Three salvage vessels extended towing cables to the ship, while pumps were "squirting thousands of gallons of salt water an hour overboard."[175]

The operation drew a crowd of onlookers, who invaded private properties along the bluffs to get a glimpse of the activities.

Among the salvage ships on site was the *Windlass*, from which a heavy steel cable was attached to the *Baldwin*. Several attempts were made to dislodge the destroyer at each high tide but the process was incredibly slow. On April 29 during one of these procedures, 20-year-old sailor, Tommie King, of Norfolk, Virginia, had been operating the cable winch when the four-inch cable snapped, whipping back and hitting him in the head, killing him instantly. Another sailor, Charles McCoy of Philadelphia, suffered a broken leg in the same accident and was taken to Southampton Hospital.

Following this tragedy were setbacks from weather conditions, which caused nearly a week's delay. Then some equipment was lost when ships left the scene to go to Fort Pond Bay, necessitating a trip to New London for replacements. On May 29, the Navy declared that it would cost more to remove the *Baldwin* than it was worth, so the decision was made to scuttle it out in the Atlantic.

Finally, on June 5, 1961, one day before the 17th anniversary of its participation in the D-Day invasion at Normandy, the U.S.S. *Baldwin* was finally removed from the shores of Montauk, towed 90 miles southeast, and left to sink in about 1,200 feet of water. If the incident hadn't occurred, the destroyer was doomed anyway, having been taken out of service back in 1946 and recently destined to be scrapped at the Boston Navy Yard.

Joshua B (1961)

On August 29, 1961, the *Joshua B*, a 63-foot Montauk fishing party boat with 54 persons aboard, under Capt. Lester Behan, was struck amidships by the 50-foot commercial fishing craft *Anna Grace* in thick fog near Southwest Ledge buoy, midway between Montauk Point and Block Island. The *Joshua B* quickly filled with water.

The *Anna Grace*, out of Point Judith, Rhode Island, pulled alongside and tied to the sinking vessel, enabling most of the passengers — women and children first — to leap aboard. Since all passengers had donned life jackets, there were no casualties. The Coast Guard from Block Island also assisted in picking up survivors. The *Joshua B* went down in 15 minutes.

Due to the heavy fog prevailing, the *Joshua B* was one of the few boats to put out from Montauk that morning at 6 a.m. The collision took place about an hour and a half later.

U.S.S. Baldwin (right) being refloated off Montauk Point 1961
(U.S. Navy)

At the time of the collision, six-foot waves prevailed, with visibility only about 50 yards. The radar aboard the *Anna Grace* was not working, and just before it struck, a passenger aboard the *Joshua B* described it as "like a ghost ship looming out at us; there was nobody visible on it when it hit."[176]

Another passenger said,

> The seas seemed 10 feet high. The fog was deep. Visibility was zero. From out of nowhere a fishing boat hit us amidships on the port side. It cracked us wide open — right down through the deck. Capt. Behan's son Jimmy, the first mate, handed out life jackets to all of us and we started going across to the Anna Grace. The two women and five children got off first. Then the rest of us started across. All but 15 of us were on the fishing boat when the Joshua started

to capsize. We jumped into the water and the crew of the Anna Grace started picking us up, one by one. Captain Behan held up an injured man until they both were picked up.

Just before I got on the Anna Grace the bow of the Joshua rose up and then she slid down out of sight in the water — she sank quickly.[177]

The *Anna Grace* took the passengers to Block Island where they were given breakfast and blankets at the Narragansett Inn. By nightfall they were all returned to Montauk aboard another vessel.

Many agreed that there was, for the most part, a prevailing sense of calm throughout the entire ordeal which helped prevent a worse situation. "It was more than a miracle, it was luck, the work and aid of the passengers themselves, and the crew of the *Anna Grace*,"[178] said Captain Behan.

An investigation of the incident found Capt. Raymond Browning, skipper of the *Anna Grace*, negligent because of his failure to post a lookout in his ship's bow, which is "required by the section of the International and Inland Rules of the Road that covers poor visibility."[179]

Felicite (1961)

In the early morning hours of September 4, 1961, the 27-foot racing sloop *Felicite* ran aground on the rocks between False Point and Jones Reef, after the crew had apparently mistaken the Montauk Lighthouse for one on Block Island. Coast Guard personnel at the Montauk Lighthouse reported the boat hit shortly after midnight in thick fog.

The crew came ashore safely and sought aid at the Lighthouse. Coast Guardsmen from Station Montauk at Star Island dragged the boat out to sea, but severe damage from the grounding caused it to sink. Stewart Lester of Amagansett managed to salvage only the mast.

Ricky E (1963)

"Extremely lucky" were the words used to describe the three passengers aboard the 26-foot cabin cruiser *Ricky E*, which capsized and disappeared just southeast of the Montauk Lighthouse on the night of October 12, 1963.

Three separate waves struck the vessel, the first of which washed Max Tannenbaum, the owner, overboard. He had been fishing in the stern. Then the second wave knocked the boat over. A third swamped the boat completely, sending the other two people into the water. They grabbed hold of a seat cushion and "rode it ashore like a surfboard,"[180] according to police.

Meanwhile, Tannenbaum swam safely ashore and was taken to the Lighthouse by surfcasters. The other two made it safely into Turtle Cove, just below the Lighthouse.

All were treated at the Lighthouse for shock and submersion.

The *Ricky E* was a total loss. But, according to East Hampton Town Police Chief William C. Jacobs, "They were out fishing again the next day in another boat. You've got to hand it to them."[181]

Unnamed vessel (1967)

A small 15-foot fishing boat capsized about six miles off Montauk Point on August 20, 1967, with the loss of 5 of its 6 passengers.

The Coast Guard said that six people aboard such a small boat was considered dangerous. However, the boat's owner, Henry Uihlein, had rented the craft with the understanding that only four passengers (a safe limit in his estimation) would be going out. Said Uihlein,

> *If all aboard had been near the stern, waves would have washed over it and filled it. The boat was in perfect condition, unless they hit a rock out there. We always give safety instructions about how far to go and how to operate the motor, but we don't know what they do after they get out there.*[182]

Uihlein added that the boat was equipped with four Coast Guard-approved lifesavers.

The lone survivor, Edward Roberts of Brooklyn, was picked up by a cabin cruiser after he had been clinging to the boat for two hours. He said later, "We got lost in the fog and we started taking water … It sprung a leak. So much water came in we capsized. The others just disappeared one at a time … I saw four disappear under the water."[183]

Viking Star (1968)

The party fishing boat *Viking Star*, out of Montauk, broke up on rocks known as "The Churches" in heavy fog, about 600 feet west of the Montauk Lighthouse at 3:30 p.m. in the afternoon of March 11, 1968. All 40 aboard reached shore safely.

A local resident spotted the fishermen struggling onto the beach and contacted the Montauk Fire Department, which brought rescue equipment and blankets, and transported them back to the fire station.

The boat's captain, Carl Forsberg, was returning with a full day's catch when the accident occurred. Once the ship hit the rocks and began breaking apart, Forsberg ordered an evacuation. Most suffered cuts and bruises in the process.

The *Viking Star* was a total loss.

Sojourn (1972)

The 30-foot sloop *Sojourn* came ashore at Hither Hills State Park in the early evening of April 6, 1972. The two young men aboard believed they were in a harbor. After grounding they swam ashore and spent the night at the Wavecrest Motel in Montauk. They were located there next morning after the boat had been discovered and a search for the two men had begun.

The men had embarked on a pleasure cruise from Noank, Connecticut, and had come ashore in a dinghy at Two Mile Hollow Beach, East Hampton, seeking provisions. Once under way, the dinghy sank, and the sloop's auxiliary engine failed.

The sloop was hauled off on April 8 and taken to the Montauk Marine Basin for minor repairs.

Atlantic Cape (1972)

The *Atlantic Cape*, an 80-foot lobster boat, broke loose from its moorings at Duryea's Dock in Fort Pond Bay in almost gale-force winds, and wound up on the beach near the New York Ocean Science Laboratory on June 10, 1972. The only crewman aboard was unable to maneuver the vessel in such adverse conditions and instead abandoned ship and ran for help.

The boat suffered no damage and was hauled off the following evening by George Glas's *Hel-Cat*, with assistance from a Coast Guard Station Montauk vessel.

The Atlantic Cape, aground at Fort Pond Bay, 1972
(Montauk Library)

Stormy Weather (1974)

The 83-foot commercial fishing trawler *Stormy Weather* of Stonington, Connecticut, began taking on water on the evening of April 7, 1974, and began to sink two miles east of Montauk Point.

Once notified, the Coast Guard sent a helicopter, which lowered three pumps to aid in the removal of the water. However, it was to no avail, and the three men aboard, all from Noank, Connecticut, abandoned ship less than a half-hour later and boarded a life raft in 10-foot seas. They were picked up by the *Rose Mary*, another trawler from Stonington, which had picked up the distress signal and sailed toward the endangered vessel.

Dragnet (1974)

On the evening of June 22, 1974, two fishing boats from North Carolina collided in dense fog about two miles northeast of Montauk Point. The 68-foot trawler, *Dragnet*, sank quickly, shortly after being hit by the *Miss Maxine*.

All four crewmen aboard the *Dragnet* were rescued by another fishing boat in the area, the *Ida K*.

The Coast Guard cutter *Point Wells* was dispatched from Station Montauk and assisted with the pumping of the *Miss Maxine*, which sustained a few holes in its bow in the collision. It was towed to Montauk Harbor and later escorted to Greenport for repairs to its hull.

Amazon (1978)

The *Amazon*, a 73-foot, 58-ton steel-hulled racing yawl built in Southampton, England, and headed from Antigua to Newport, Rhode Island, for summer races, ran on the rocks at Dead Man's Cove, Ditch Plain, in the early morning hours of May 8, 1978. The $500,000 vessel became engulfed by fog and was driven ashore by the tides. It was later dragged ashore.

Bruce Muir, son of the boat's owner, Mrs. Robert Muir (and a great-nephew of the American naturalist John Muir), in charge of the vessel at the time, said, "What can you say? The fog was so thick you couldn't see the bow."[184] At one point the fog was so thick that the Coast Guard boat was only 150 feet away from the *Amazon* and still couldn't see it.

Efforts to refloat the *Amazon* took much longer than expected. Early attempts proved ineffective. A tug from Costello's Marine Constructing Corporation of Greenport tried first. Then two draggers, the *Mary Moon* and the *Patricia E*, failed, losing several tow lines in the process.

By May 10 the actions of the tide and waves pushed the *Amazon* to within 50 feet of the beach and it was reportedly full of water.

It was then decided to move the *Amazon* landward instead. On May 13 the Bistrian Sand and Gravel Corporation took four heavy duty trucks and a crane and dragged it off the rocks in preparation for the vessel to be transported overland to a boatyard in Mamaroneck, New York, for repairs. However, the Muir's insurance company thought otherwise, so it was decided to make the trip by water.

> *[A]n attempt will be made to drag her down to the beach to a point where the water is deep enough to launch her, and to tow her by tug to Mamaroneck. She was dismasted yesterday, and is to be patched up, sealed, and fitted with a new rudder before her voyage, which is not expected to occur sooner than a week from now.*[185]

According to *The East Hampton Star*, the *Amazon*, built in 1971, "was made whole again" at Mamaroneck, continued racing, was sold a number of times, and as of 2013 was "cruising the Mediterranean."[186]

Calypso (1979)

On July 22, 1979, the *Calypso*, a 43-foot yawl heading for Sag Harbor from Atlantic City, New Jersey, ran on the rocks at Ditch Plain in dense fog, at the same location as the *Amazon* the year before. Capt. Tom Harris of Camden, New Jersey, and all four passengers made it safely to shore.

The boat began to fill with water immediately after striking the rocks and sustained considerable damage. It was removed by truck a few days later.

Elizabeth R (1979)

The 93-foot seascalloper, *Elizabeth R*, after suffering engine trouble while at sea, was towed into Fort Pond Bay on December 14, 1979, and moored at the New York Ocean Science Laboratory dock. Three days later, in mid-afternoon, during a northwester, the vessel lost its moorings, spun 180 degrees, and ran up on the beach, causing extensive damage to its hull, severely damaging the dock, and knocking out the electricity at the laboratory. No one was aboard at the time.

The Long Island Lighting Company was able to restore power to the laboratory within two hours.

About an hour after the grounding, the ship's captain, Donald Hawthorne, and two of his crewmen succeeded in easing the vessel back into the water. However, this was not the end of the story. Senior Chief Gary Samuelson, commander of Station Montauk, reported that about an hour and a half later, when the Coast Guard radioed the vessel "to find out how she was doing, her crew told us she was taking on water very fast and sinking. The crew reported that her engine was almost underwater and that they were going to beach her, which they did," to the west of the Laboratory dock.[187]

The Coast Guard responded, as did over 40 men from the Montauk Fire Department. Fire Chief Craig Tuthill said, "Waves were crashing over the boat and dock … It was so cold out there, the spray turned to ice immediately."[188]

The ship's crew was removed safely from the boat. According to Coast Guard Chief Samuelson, they endured a "wind chill factor of minus 21 degrees, were cold and wet, but otherwise fine; they required no medical attention and were taken to the Montauk Fire House for a good hot shower."[189]

The ship's owner, Joseph Rha, of Philadelphia, was informed of the situation and told it was up to him to remove the *Elizabeth R* from the beach.

Elizabeth R ashore in Fort Pond Bay, Montauk, 1979
(Montauk Library)

Minnie (1981)

On October 28, 1981, the *Minnie*, a 36-foot wooden workboat, while in rough seas south of Montauk Point, suffered engine failure and radioed for help. The Coast Guard from Montauk responded and began towing the boat toward Montauk Harbor. As they rounded Montauk Point, the boat began taking on water. Coast Guardsmen managed to get a pump to the *Minnie* but it was no use. About 45 minutes later, the boat sank.

Don Ball of East Hampton, the owner and skipper, and his crewman were rescued. The cause of the sinking was undetermined.

Sophie G (1982)

The *Sophie G*, a 70-foot steel-hulled lobster boat out of Stonington, Connecticut, carrying a full load of fresh-caught lobster, ran aground in rainy, foggy weather about a half-mile south of the Montauk Lighthouse on April 27, 1982. Since the New Bedford tug *Jaguar* was unable to get close enough to the boat, the Coast Guard at Station Montauk was able to remove the stranded vessel and return it to Connecticut.

Petty Officer Paul Driscoll, officer in charge at the Lighthouse, said the Coast Guard "made the difference between salvage and disaster." Five of the six aboard the boat ended up spending the night at the Lighthouse. The remaining man, said Officer Driscoll, "was insistent. We kept a live beach watch on him overnight."[190]

It was determined that there were no holes in the vessel, though Officer Driscoll noted, "it did have some dents and crinkles."[191]

Wind Blown (1984)

The fishing boat *Wind Blown*, a 65-foot steel-hulled longliner with a crew of four, left Montauk on March 22, 1984, for a weeklong fishing trip in the Atlantic Canyon, over 120 miles southeast of Montauk. Aboard were David Connick, Michael Vigilant, and Scott Clark, all of Montauk, and Michael Stedman, the captain, from East Hampton. Contact was last made with the men at 7 a.m. on March 29 when it was on its way home, about 12 miles southeast of Montauk Point and apparently encountering severe stormy conditions.

A relative of Stedman's notified the Coast Guard when it was clear that the men were definitely late in returning. The Coast Guard conducted a check of all marinas from Fire Island to Cape Cod for any word of the missing vessel. There was none.

> *The Shinnecock station was notified of an EPIRB (emergency position indicating radio beacon — a floating beacon activated and released by a ship in distress) picked up that evening by the 82-foot Coast Guard Cutter Point Wells dispatched from Montauk to investigate. The cutter searched for the beacon in 15 to 18 foot seas for seven hours with negative results. Winds at the time were 60 knots, gusting to 80 knots.*[192]

The Coast Guard began a search of the area. Station Shinnecock sent four boats, three helicopters and two planes. Station Montauk utilized their cutter *Point Wells*, which turned up wreckage and debris about 18 miles south of Shinnecock Inlet, including paddles inscribed "Windblown." Even private fishing vessels found wreckage that was identified as belonging to the lost vessel. The *Viking Star* brought in a section of the pilothouse decking,

> *which was put into a storage area at the Montauk Coast Guard Station where a growing pile of debris testified to the unfolding story of a tragedy at sea. The orange cork life raft and paddles of the Windblown…lay beneath part of a broken-up bulkhead, a section of the pilothouse decking, several interior walls, a chart table, and a pilothouse door, all identified as belonging to the missing boat. The EPIRB picked up Friday morning 15 miles south of Shinnecock Inlet…was identified as belonging to the Windblown.*[193]

The search area was extended from Montauk Point to Great Egg Inlet, south of Cape May, New Jersey. However, on April 2, the Coast Guard called off the search, their efforts impeded by six to eight foot–seas and snowy conditions.

About 400 jammed Most Holy Trinity Church in East Hampton for the funeral Mass for Stedman and Connick on April 12.

The names of the four missing fishermen are part of the list of engraved names on the Lost at Sea Memorial at the Montauk Point Lighthouse.

Anne Louise (1993)

The 35-foot fishing trawler *Anne Louise* had embarked on its maiden voyage with its new owner, Joe Hodnik, and his crewman, Ed Sabo, both from Montauk, on March 2, 1993. Early next morning the boat issued a distress call while 25 miles south of Martha's Vineyard. By nightfall on March 4, debris from a fishing boat was discovered about 25 miles south of Montauk, but there was no sign of either of the 26-year-old fishermen.

Coast Guardsmen from several areas responded, finding floating bait boxes filled with fresh bait. Coast Guard aircraft and one from the Suffolk Air National Guard and a Coast Guard cutter began a massive search. Additional debris was discovered but still no sign of the young men.

The Coast Guard considered suspending the search since weather conditions had deteriorated. However, said Coast Guard Petty Officer Greg Robinson, "We are still searching based on the premise that they may have a life raft."[194]

By March 6 the search was suspended on the premise that it was unlikely the fishermen could have survived to that point, despite finding additional debris and an oil slick. However, said Hodnik's father, Joe, "Until I see for sure with my own eyes that he didn't make it, there's always hope."[195] It was not to be.

The names of Hodnik and Sabo were engraved into the marble base of the Lost at Sea Memorial, located on the grounds of the Montauk Point Lighthouse.

Serena (2006)

The *Serena*, a 55-foot scallop boat owned by Adam Rathbun of North Stonington, Connecticut, and leaking diesel fuel, ran aground on the rocks about a mile and a half west of the Montauk Lighthouse on June 1, 2006. The two crewmen aboard got off safely. The Coast Guard, led by Senior Chief Nicholas Pupo, contained the spill. The Miller Environmental Group from Calverton, Long Island, were able to remove the fuel tanks before the ship broke up.

The boat was declared a total loss and later dragged out to sea by the Coast Guard and scuttled.

Johanna Lenore (2011)

A Coast Guard helicopter took the four-man crew off of the quickly-sinking *Johanna Lenore*, a 72-foot fishing trawler, which capsized after taking on water about 40 miles south of Montauk on January 18, 2011. They were taken to Cape Cod for evaluation by medical personnel.

The crew had been hurriedly pumping gallons of water out of the ship, but the pumps could not keep pace with the flow of water coming in.

A distress call was sent to Coast Guard Sector Long Island Sound's command center, which sent a helicopter from the Cape Cod air station.

A 47-foot motor lifeboat was also dispatched from Station Montauk.

Anna Mary – fisherman John Aldridge (2013)

On July 24, 2013, Montauk fisherman John Aldridge fell overboard into shark-infested waters from the fishing boat *Anna Mary* around 3:30 a.m., about 60 miles south of Montauk. Once discovered missing by a fellow crewman, Anthony Sosinski, the Coast Guard was contacted and sent out two rescue patrol boats, aircraft and two rescue helicopters. They were aided in the operation by numerous Montauk fishermen who, "basically stopped what they were doing and headed in my direction," said Sosinski.[196]

After a nearly 12-hour search Aldridge was found about 45 miles south of Montauk by an Air Station Cape Cod MH-60 Jayhawk helicopter crew. Though clad in only a pair of shorts, T-shirt, and possibly socks, he was alert. It was noted that he wore no life jacket when he first fell overboard. Aldridge claimed that his rubber boats acted as floatation devices and saved his life.

Station Montauk commander Jason Walter was amazed at the outcome. "I guess I have to remember to be an optimist. You hear of this down south where the water is warmer but it's different up here."[197] He also said, "The search and rescue coordination between the Coast Guard, its partner agencies, and fishermen was exceptional. The fishing crews allowed us to search a much greater area. To find this man in the water after this much time is amazing."[198]

For their efforts in rescuing Aldridge, members of Coast Guard Station Montauk received the Meritorious Team Commendation in December. Said Capt. Edward Cubanski, commander of Sector Long Island Sound, who made the presentation, "The devotion to duty and the outstanding performance demonstrated by Station Montauk are in keeping with the highest traditions of the United States Coast Guard."[199]

Margaret Mary (2015)

On November 28, 2015, the *Margaret Mary*, a commercial fishing boat, owned by the Fridenberger family, and captained by Roy Fridenberger, bound from Montauk to Freeport, Long Island, grounded after it began taking on water. It was making its last voyage of the season before docking for the winter at Inlet Seafood in Montauk.

Only two miles off Montauk shores, the vessel began taking on water. The Coast Guard was contacted, who directed them to beach the vessel at an area of Napeague that was free of rocks. The landing was successful and not one of the 150 gallons of diesel fuel that had just been put into the tank was lost, nor were there any injuries.

Next day, Fridenberger and family came to view the stranded vessel, which was partially buried in sand. The captain began the task of removing the boat that day with help from his seven brothers and five sisters, many of whom lived in the Mastic Beach-Shirley area of Long Island.

Captain Fridenberger expected to float the craft by December 7.

CHAPTER 9

Lost at Sea Memorial

IN 1994 APPROXIMATELY 15 individuals, some of whom had lost relatives in boating catastrophes in the last several years, formed the Lost at Sea Memorial Committee, dedicating itself to the creation of a powerful and solemn monument to forever remember those fishermen whose lives were lost at sea.

A competition was held for the best sculpture to represent the fishermen, and in May 1996, a 60-inch model, designed by artist Malcolm Frazier, was unveiled at Gosman's Dock Restaurant in Montauk before a group of East End fishermen, town officials, and Montauk residents. The committee unanimously accepted the model, which depicted an eight-foot-tall fisherman standing in a dory, resting atop a seven-foot granite base, which was to have the names of the lost fishermen engraved into it.

When it was suggested to Frazier that the number of commercial fishermen appeared to be declining in recent years, Frazier said of his creation, "The monument's purpose is to honor the people lost at sea. But, I definitely hoped when I designed it that it would be a monument to the industry. I hope it isn't a memorial to it."[200]

Work on the memorial began at the Polich Art Works foundry in Newburgh, New York, in January 1999.

The granite base was donated by Granite Works in Deer Park, Long Island. Its president, Elaine d'Angeleo, said, "I thought this was a way to honor these brave fishermen, who are often underappreciated but who are the backbone of Long Island's heritage."[201]

In February the search was on for the names of fishermen from the five easternmost Suffolk towns who had died at sea in the last 50 years.

Said Arnold Leo, a member of the committee and secretary of the East Hampton Baymen's Association, "This memorial is really a tribute to the men and women who go to sea to earn a living. But the memorial is really most important for the survivors, the families who've never recovered any remains and therefore have no place to go to remember their loved ones."[202]

The site for the monument was donated by the Montauk Historical Society, on the last possible level piece of ground on Long Island, atop a cliff overlooking Block Island Sound and the Atlantic Ocean on the property of the Montauk Point Lighthouse. Local fishermen and their families favored the decision. Dick White, a member of the committee and chairman of the Lighthouse Committee of the Montauk Historical Society, said, "This is a perfect spot for this memorial, since it will be prominently displayed on the cliff of this famous Lighthouse, which has stood watch over Montauk waters since its construction in 1796."[203] When completed, the monument would be maintained by the Town of East Hampton.

Meanwhile, a drive was on to raise funds for the monument, with considerable support coming from designer Ralph Lauren ($30,000) and singer Billy Joel ($15,000). By February 1999, $200,000 had been raised toward the $225,000 cost.

A LEGACY OF VALOR

The Lost at Sea Memorial was dedicated on October 10, 1999. At that time, the names of lost fishermen, dating back to 1937, had been engraved on its base. Praise and reflection poured out from committee members in attendance:

Roberta Gosman Donovan, owner of Gosman's Dock Restaurant in Montauk: "I think this is a dramatic statement of the fisherman's hard, unpredictable life at sea."

Anne Hodnik, whose husband Joe Hodnik went down with the fishing trawler *Anne Louise* in 1993: "At last we have a place to go and remember Joe and Ed."

Pat Lockwood, whose son Tovey Lesnikowski was lost in 1994: "We've waited five years to finally have a place to mourn and remember. I would have sacrificed everything I own to be able to have this memorial tribute to my son and his fellow fishermen. I'm so glad it's finally here."[204]

Today, the memorial contains 121 names, the four oldest dating from February 24, 1719, when Henry Parsons, William Schellinger, Jr., Lewis Mulford, and Jeremiah Conkling, Jr. were lost. Records show that "This day a whale-boat being alone the men struck a whale and she coming under ye boat in part staved it, and though ye men were not hurt with the whale yet, before any help came to them four men were tired and chilled and fell off ye boat and oars to which they hung and were drowned."[205]

The Lost at Sea Memorial continues to be a poignant reminder of the risks that fishermen take each time they venture out to sea.

Lost at Sea Memorial is shown in December 2010. The solemn monument depicts 121 names of Long Island East End commercial fishermen who lost their lives at sea around the world. (Author photo)

The Lost at Sea Memorial, shown in April 2015, is a poignant reminder of the dangers that lurk every time fishermen go to sea. (Author photo)

APPENDIX A

Keepers/Officers in Charge of Montauk Life Saving and Coast Guard Stations

Montauk Point

Jonathan A. Miller	1865-1869
Thomas Ripley	1869-1872
Jonathan A. Miller	1872-1875

Station maintained by crew of the Ditch Plain Life Saving Station thereafter.

Ditch Plain

	Service
Patrick Gould	1856 – 1859
Samuel T. Stratton	1872 – 1880
Frank S. Stratton	1880 – 1892
William B. Miller	1892 – 1903
Carl H. Hedges	1903 – 1916
Russell Garfield Miller	1916 – 1918
Knowles H. Smith	1918 – 1924
Frank D. Warner	1928 – 1931
Lloyd Starrin	1931 – 1933
Earl M. Pike	1933 – 1937
John M. Odin	1937 – 1939
Charles W. O'Neil	1939 – 1945

Hither Plain

	Service
John B. Lawrence	1869 – 1873
George H. Osborne	1872 – 1881
George E. Filer	1881 – 1891
William D. Parsons	1892 – 1917
Hiram F. King	1917 – 1920
Keeper position vacant	1920 – 1922
Station closed	1922 – 1925
Jetur Reeve Harlow	1925 – 1930
Cecil Wessels	1930 – 1931
Earl M. Pike	1931 – 1933
William Hawley — caretaker	1933 – 1937
Station closed	1933 – 1941

Coast Guard Station Montauk

Leslie Furst	1955 – 1961
John Cherney	1961 – 1965
Robert Gedlick	1965
Steve Allen	1977
Gary Samuelson	1979
Pete Weihermuller	1979-1986
Steven Loncar	1980s
Michael Bagnato	1980s
Dennis Harper	1982
Edward Michels	1986 – 1989
John Dusch	1989 – 1993
Paul F. Casey	1993 – 1994
Donald Cavanaugh	1994 – 1999
Dennis Endicott	1999 – 2003
Nicholas Pupo	2003 – 2006
James Weber	2006 – 2009
Gordon McClay (temporary)	2009 – 2010
Jason Walter	2010 – 2015
Eric Best	2015 -

APPENDIX B

Lost at Sea Memorial Inscriptions

	Name	Missing	Age
1	Jeremiah Conkling	February 24, 1719	24
2	Lewis Mulford	February 24, 1719	26
3	Henry Parsons	February 24, 1719	29
4	William Skellinx	February 24, 1719	24
5	Dick	January 17, 1753	
6	Daniel Baker	January 17, 1753	61
7	Jacob Skellinx	January 17, 1753	51
8	Capt. Clarke's Son	1766	
9	Henry Miller	1770	
10	Henry Miller	1775	
11	John Hand	January 25, 1826	31
12	Theodorus Miller	January 15, 1830	19
13	Jonathan Miller	March 1834	14
14	Collins King	April 19, 1834	
15	Daniel Brown	October 10, 1834	
16	David Leek	October 10, 1834	25
17	Erastus Halsey	October 10, 1834	
18	William Schellenger	October 10, 1834	28
19	Samuel Ludlow	October 10, 1834	
20	Charles Howell	October 10, 1834	
21	Sylvester Stanborough	October 10, 1834	
22	Henry Miller	October 10, 1834	
23	Benjamin Payne	October 10, 1834	
24	Edward Jennings	October 10, 1834	
25	Edward Glover	January 14, 1836	29
26	Abraham Osborn	January 1, 1838	30
27	Charles Payne	January 4, 1838	30
28	Richard Topping	February 1, 1838	
29	Stratton Harlow	October 31, 1838	27
30	John Howell	July 23, 1840	28
31	George Mulford	February 6, 1842	23

32	George Perry	1842	
33	Oliver Nickerson	July 28, 1843	25
34	Isaac Post	1843	
35	Johiel Penny	June 28, 1843	
36	Isaac Platt	February 6, 1845	
37	Charles Isaacs	July 1845	41
38	David V. R. Conkling	July 1845	41
39	William Pierson	June 1, 1846	30
40	Jonathan Salmon	December 5, 1847	
41	Manuel Oliver	August 1848	
42	Samuel Coles	1850	
43	George Brown	1853	
44	Robert Weeks	May 1, 1856	23
45	Emmett Osborne	1856	
46	Charles Bennett	July 1857	25
47	William Bennett	July 1857	25
48	James Hamilton	1866	
49	Samuel Reeves	1866	
50	William Fowler	1866	
51	Jeremiah Loper	1866	
52	Edward Fowler	1866	
53	J. A. Fields	1866	
54	John Rhoderick	1866	
55	Thomas Aldridge	1866	
56	Thomas Higgins	1866	
57	R. B. Vernon	1866	
58	Alex Schultz	1866	
59	P. Mettz	1866	
60	G. Stertof	1866	
61	W. A. Bachr	1866	
62	F. J. Morton	1866	
63	A. McDonald	1866	
64	Edward Parker	1866	
65	A. Bronce	1866	
66	H. Dugan	1866	
67	T. J. Seeley	1866	
68	W. J. Johnson	1866	
69	S. A. Howard	1866	
70	Thomas Lee	1866	
71	Bob Kanaka	1866	
72	Joseph Menday	November 1868	
73	Milton Tryon	November 1868	
74	Albert Edwards	December 18, 1873	

LOST AT SEA MEMORIAL INSCRIPTIONS

75	Moses Walker	October 15, 1885	
76	Ferdinand Lee	October 15, 1885	
77	W. M. Garrison Lee	October 15, 1885	
78	Wilber King	December 5, 1902	29
79	Oscar Berg	December 9, 1915	35
80	Nathaniel Edwards	February 19, 1937	22
81	Benjamin Tuthill	August 21, 1938	48
82	Jesse Hodge	September 21, 1938	
83	David Starvi	September 21, 1938	
84	Elton Smith	September 21, 1938	
85	Samuel Coleman	September 21, 1938	
86	Kermit Forsett	September 21, 1938	
87	Roy Griffin	September 21, 1938	
88	Samuel Edwards	September 21, 1938	35
89	Vivian Smith	September 21, 1938	30
90	Herbert Fields	September 21, 1938	36
91	Gilbert Edwards	September 21, 1938	30
92	Claude Burrows	September 21, 1938	
93	Seth Scribner	September 21, 1938	30
94	William Dunn	September 22, 1949	51
95	Edward Carroll	September 1, 1951	33
96	Kenneth Lester	April 26, 1952	30
97	Fred Tonner	September 24, 1953	57
98	Eugene Anderson	December 10, 1960	28
99	William Anderson Jr.	December 10, 1960	32
100	Claude Malliet	November 12, 1978	31
101	Raymond Banks	November 12, 1978	23
102	Richard Vigilante	November 12, 1978	42
103	Victor Crump	November 30, 1980	28
104	Michael Vigilante	March 29, 1984	19
105	David Connick	March 29, 1984	23
106	Scott Clark	March 29, 1984	19
107	Michael Stedman	March 29, 1984	32
108	Edward Trufanoff	May 12, 1985	33
109	Sidney Havens	May 12, 1985	57
110	Thomas Anderson	April 11, 1988	45
111	Scott Gates	November 20, 1989	21
112	Matthew MacKey	June 24, 1990	23
113	Herbert Zickmund	May 4, 1992	63
114	Edmund Sabo	March 3, 1993	27
115	Joseph Hodnik	March 3, 1993	26
116	Herman Wendel	November 8, 1993	40
117	Tovey Lesnikowski	October 9, 1994	34

118	John Grimley	December 30, 1995	44
119	Norman Edwards	May 16, 1997	76
120	William Myers	February 21, 1996	41
121	James Szekely	November 29, 1998	51

Bibliography

Annual Report of the Operations of the United States Life-Saving Service for the Fiscal Year Ending June 30, 1877. Washington: Government Printing Office, 1877.

Annual Report of the United States Life-Saving Service for the Fiscal Year Ended June 30, 1882. Washington: Government Printing Office, 1883.

Annual Report of the United States Life-Saving Service for the Fiscal Year Ended June 30, 1912. Washington: Government Printing Office, 1913.

Annual Report of the United States Life-Saving Service for the Fiscal Year Ended June 30, 1913. Washington: Government Printing Office, 1914.

Appleton's Annual Cyclopedia and Register of Important Events of the Year 1878. Vol. III. New York: D. Appleton and Company, 1883.

Clavin, Tom, *Dark Noon; the Final Voyage of the Fishing Boat 'Pelican.'* New York: International Marine-McGraw Hill, 2005.

Clowes, Ernest S., *The Hurricane of 1938 on Eastern Long Island.* Bridgehampton: Hampton Press, 1939.

Foster, Sherrill, "Two Shipwrecks." In *Revealing the Past; the Historical Works Regarding East Hampton, New York of Norton Daniels, Sherrill Foster, Mac Griswold, and Hugh King."* Tom Twomey (ed). Bridgehampton: East End Press, 2014.

Gish, Noel, "Pirates." In *Awakening the Past; the East Hampton 350th Anniversary Lecture Series 1998."* Tom Twomey (ed). New York: Newmarket Press, 1999.

Hedges, Henry P. *A History of the Town of East Hampton, N. Y.* Sag Harbor: J. H. Hunt, 1897.

Keatts, Henry, George Farr. *The Bell Tolls: Shipwrecks and Lighthouses; Volume 2, Eastern Long Island.* Homosassa, Fla: Fathom Press, 2002.

Kimball, Sumner. *Organization and Methods of the United States Life-Saving Service.* Washington: Government Printing Office, 1912.

Lanman, Charles. *Recollections of Curious Characters and Pleasant Places.* Edinburgh: Thomas and Archibald Constable, 1881.

The Master, Mate and Pilot. New York: American Association of Masters, Mates and Pilots, June 1908.

Means, Dennis R. "A Heavy Sea Running: The Formation of the U. S. Life-Saving Service 1846-1878." in *Prologue Magazine,* winter 1987, Vol. 19, No. 4.

Noble, Dennis. *That Others Might Live: The U. S. Life-Saving Service 1878-1915.* Annapolis: Naval Institute Press, 1994.

Official Register of the United States, Containing a List of Officers and Employees in the Civil, Military, and Naval Service on the First of July, 1885, Vol. I. Washington: Government Printing Office. 1885.

Osmers, Henry. *American Gibraltar: Montauk and the Wars of America.* Denver: Outskirts Press, 2011.

Osmers, Henry. *Living on the Edge: Life at the Montauk Point Lighthouse 1930-1945.* Denver: Outskirts Press, 2009.

Osmers, Henry. *On Eagle's Beak: A History of the Montauk Point Lighthouse.* Denver: Outskirts Press, 2008.

Osmers, Henry. *They Were All Strangers: The Wreck of the John Milton at Montauk, New York.* Denver: Outskirts Press, 2010.

Overton, Jacqueline. *Long Island's Story* (Port Washington: Ira J. Friedman, Inc., 1963).

Rattray, Jeannette Edwards. *Ship Ashore!* New York: Coward-McCann Inc., 1955.

Register of Officers and Agents, Civil, Military, and Naval, in the Service of the United States on the Thirtieth of September, 1873. Washington: Government Printing Office, 1874.

Report of the Operations of the United States Life-Saving Service for the Fiscal Year Ending June 30, 1876. Washington: Government Printing Office, 1876.

Sailor's Magazine and Seamen's Friend. New York: American Seamen's Friend Society, October 1871.

Sheard, Bradley. *Lost Voyages.* New York: Aqua Quest Publications.

Willoughby, Malcolm F. *The U. S. Coast Guard in World War II.* Annapolis: Naval Institute Press, 1957.

Newspapers

Binghamton Press
Brooklyn Daily Eagle
County Review (Suffolk County)
Dan's Papers
East Hampton Star
Long Islander
Mid-Island Mail
New York Daily News
New York Daily Tribune
New York Herald Tribune
New York Sun
New York Times
New York Tribune
Newsday
Patchogue Advance
Port Jefferson Echo
Sag Harbor Corrector
Sag Harbor Express
Salt Lake Herald
South Side Signal
Suffolk County News
Suffolk Life
Utica Daily Press
The Watchman

Miscellaneous Sources

Ditch Plain Life Saving Station Journal 1873-1878.

Henry E. Huntting Life Saving Collection.

The History Project (oral interviews). Long Island Collection, East Hampton Library.

National Archives. Record Group 26.

Speech of James W. Covert of New York in the House of Representative, March 11, 1878. Washington: 1878.

"U.S. Life Saving Service and U.S. Coast Guard Stations Located along the Coast of Long Island, NY, and their Assigned Station Rescue Boats." Compiled by Timothy R. Dring; Commander, U.S. Naval Reserve (Retired). August 2012.

Endnotes

Chapter 1 – General History of the U. S. Life Saving Service

1. Jacqueline Overton, *Long Island's Story* (Port Washington: Ira J. Friedman, Inc., 1963), 226.
2. Malcolm F. Willoughby, *The U.S. Coast Guard in World War II* (Annapolis, MD: Naval Institute Press, 1957), 4.
3. Overton, 226.
4. Overton, 227.
5. "Rescue from Wreck; Life Saving on the Long Island Coast," *Brooklyn Daily Eagle,* August 7, 1871.
6. Ibid.
7. *Report of the Operations of the United States Life-Saving Service for the Fiscal Year Ending June 30, 1876* (Washington: Government Printing Office, 1876), 35-36.
8. Speech of James W. Covert of New York in the House of Representatives, March 11, 1878. (Washington: 1878).
9. *Appleton's Annual Cyclopedia and Register of Important Events of the Year 1878, Vol. III.* (New York: D. Appleton and Company, 1883), 757.
10. Abram Loper deposition, Dec. 17, 1877, Henry E. Huntting Life Saving Collection. Long Island Collection, East Hampton Library.
11. Jonathan Payne deposition, Dec. 11, 1877, Henry E. Huntting Life-Saving Collection. Long Island Collection, East Hampton Library.
12. *Annual Report of the United States Life-Saving Service for the Fiscal Year Ended June 30, 1913* (Washington: Government Printing Office, 1914.
13. Dennis Noble, *That Others Might Live: The U.S. Life-Saving Service 1878-1915* (Annapolis: Naval Institute Press, 1994), 155.
14. Dennis R. Means, *A Heavy Sea Running: The Formation of the U. S. Life-Saving Service, 1846-1878.* Prologue Magazine, winter 1987, vol. 19, No. 4.
15. Sumner Kimball, *Organization and Methods of the United States Life-Saving Service* (Washington: Government Printing Office, 1912), 11.
16. "The Life Saving Service," *Brooklyn Daily Eagle,* September 23, 1888.
17. Jeannette Edwards Rattray, *Ship Ashore!* (New York: Coward-McCann Inc., 1955), 87-88.
18. Henry Keatts and George Farr, *The Bell Tolls: Shipwrecks and Lighthouses of Eastern Long Island* (Eastport, NY: Fathom Press, 2002), 15-16.
19. Rattray, 92.
20. Rattray, 92.

A LEGACY OF VALOR

21 *Register of Officers and Agents, Civil, Military, and Naval, in the Service of the United States on the Thirtieth of September, 1873* (Washington: Government Printing Office, 1874), 195.

22 *Official Register of the United States, Containing a List of Officers and Employees in the Civil, Military, and Naval Service on the First of July, 1885, Volume I* (Washington: Government Printing Office, 1885), 222.

23 "The Pension Bill for the Life Saving Service, *Brooklyn Daily Eagle,* May 7, 1880.

24 Noel Gish, "Pirates." In *Awakening the Past: the East Hampton 350th Anniversary Lecture Series 1998."* Tom Twomey (ed). (New York: Newmarket Press, 1999), 267.

Chapter 2 – Montauk Point Life Saving Station

25 "Life Saving Stations on Coastal New Jersey and Long Island," 1872.

26 The Raymond lifeboat was built by William Raymond in 1807 and resembled the whaleboats of the late 1700s. It was lined with cork to provide extra flotation. Thirty feet in length and manning a crew of twelve, the vessel could accommodate twenty people and performed admirably under stormy conditions.

27 Letter from Henry Huntting to Secretary of the Treasury, December 13, 1872. Henry Huntting Collection, East Hampton Library.

28 "Latest Long Island News; Life Saving Crews Increased at Midnight," *Brooklyn Daily Eagle,* December 1, 1895.

Chapter 3 – Ditch Plain Life Saving Station

29 "Life Saving Stations on Coastal New Jersey and Long Island.." 1872

30 "Miscellaneous," *Suffolk County News,* September 5, 1891.

31 1902 list courtesy of the US Life-Saving Service Heritage Association.

32 "Montauk Notes," *East Hampton Star,* October 19, 1939.

33 "Coast Guard Has Fine Record on Long Island," *East Hampton Star,* November 2, 1939.

34 Joshua Edwards deposition, December 18, 1877. Henry E. Huntting Life Saving Collection. Long Island Collection, East Hampton Library.

35 "Two Coast Guard Men Become Unruly at Ditch Plains," *East Hampton Star,* August 16, 1929.

36 "Can't Stem L.I. Rum Tide, Dry Fleet Admits," *Brooklyn Daily Eagle,* February 19, 1930.

37 "Warrant Officer Warner Advance," *East Hampton Star,* October 24, 1930.

38 "Died," *Sag Harbor Express,* August 15, 1895.

39 "Life Savers on Duty," *East Hampton Star,* August 4, 1899.

40 "Montauk Mention," *East Hampton Star,* February 11, 1910.

41 "Long Island Notes; Globe Floated Across Ocean," *Port Jefferson Echo,* September 17, 1910.

42 "Montauk," *East Hampton Star,* February 9, 1917.

43 "Village & Town News," *East Hampton Star,* May 26, 1922.

Chapter 4 – Hither Plain Life Saving Station

44 1902 list courtesy of the US Life-Saving Service Heritage Association.

45 Arthur Miller interview, October 25, 2000. The History Project. Long Island Collection, East Hampton Library.
46 "Five L.I. Stations will be Closed by the Coast Guard," *Suffolk County News*, March 12, 1937.
47 Frank Dayton interview, January 5, 1992. The History Project, Long Island Collection, East Hampton Library.
48 Henry E. Remington deposition, January 2, 1878. Henry E. Huntting Life Saving Collection. Long Island Collection, East Hampton Library.
49 Jesse Edwards deposition, December 15, 1877. Henry E. Huntting Life Saving Collection. Long Island Collection, East Hampton Library.
50 Letter to Henry E. Huntting from Charles B. Dayton, July 7, 1882. Henry E. Huntting Collection, Long Island Collection, East Hampton Library.
51 Letter to Henry E. Huntting from George E. Filer, November 13, 1884. Henry E. Huntting Collection, Long Island Collection, East Hampton Library.
52 "Farmer as well as Life Saver," *Brooklyn Daily Eagle*, February 16, 1901.
53 Capt. Parsons Retire, *East Hampton Star*, March 14, 1919.
54 "Montauk,," *East Hampton Star*, May 9, 1930.
55 Arthur Miller interview, October 25, 2000. The History Project. Long Island Collection, East Hampton Library.
56 "Montauk," *East Hampton Star*, January 22, 1887.
57 Ibid.
58 "Montauk," *East Hampton Star*, May 12, 1916.

Chapter 5 – U. S. Coast Guard Station Montauk

59 "Coast Guard Beach Patrol Finis; Radar, Loran and 'Duck' Take Over," *New York Times*, January 19, 1951.
60 "Coast Guard Putting New Lifeboats on Duty," *The Watchman*, November 11, 1965.

Chapter 6 - Notable Shipwrecks – 1600s-1877

61 Rattray, 13.
62 Rattray, 13.
63 Rattray, 16.
64 Rattray, 17-18.
65 Henry Osmers, *American Gibraltar: Montauk and the Wars of America* (Denver: Outskirts Press, 2011), 11.
66 "Historic Long Island; Wreck Named Culloden Point," *Long Islander*, October 1, 1959.
67 Bradley Sheard, *Lost Voyages* (New York; Aqua Quest Publications, 1998), 17.
68 "Brig Peggy Wrecked at Montauk in 1786," *East Hampton Star*, August 3, 1961.
69 "Shipwreck," *Corrector*, December 13, 1823.
70 Untitled, *Corrector*, March 25, 1826.
71 Henry P. Hedges, *A History of the Town of East Hampton, N.Y.* (Sag Harbor; J. H. Hunt, 1897), 153.
72 "Disasters," *New York Daily Tribune*, October 19, 1842.
73 Untitled, *Corrector*, April 24, 1852.

74 "Government Light-Boat Wrecked," *New York Daily Tribune*.

75 "The Storm Sunday; Loss of Brig Flying Cloud at Montauk," Sag Harbor Corrector, December 17, 1856.

   * Translation: "live happily venturing reserved."

76 Charles Lanman, *Recollections of Curious Characters and Pleasant Places* (Edinburgh: Thomas and Archibald Constable, 1881), 129.

77 Henry Osmers, *They Were All Strangers: The Wreck of the John Milton at Montauk, New York* (Denver: Outskirts Press, 2010), 23.

78 Ibid, 26.

79 Ibid, 29.

80 Ibid, 29-30.

81 Ibid, 44.

82 Ibid, 61-62.

83 "A Reminiscence of the Lost Ship John Milton," *Sag Harbor Express*, February 20, 1890.

84 "Vessel Ashore," *Corrector*, February 8, 1862.

85 "The Great Eastern; How the Mammoth Ship was Repaired," *New York Times*, December 17, 1862.

86 "The Great Eastern; How the Big Vessel was Used and Finally Disposed Of," *Salt Lake Herald*, January 24, 1892.

87 Rattray, 110.

88 Walt Whitman, "The Year of Meteors," 1859, 1860.

89 "Steamer Ashore," *Corrector*, October 26, 1867.

90 Untitled, *Corrector*, March 7, 1868.

91 "A Dreadful Fate; Burned to Death at Sea," *Brooklyn Daily Eagle*, October 6, 1871..

92 Journal of Ditch Plain Station, December 19, 1873. Henry Huntting Collection, East Hampton Library.

93 Journal of Ditch Plain Station, December 20, 1873. Henry Huntting Collection, East Hampton Library.

94 Journal of Hither Plain Station, December 21, 1873. Henry Huntting Collection, East Hampton Library.

95 "Montauk," *Long Island Traveler*, December 25, 1873.

96 "A Mystery of Montauk," *South Side Signal*, July 8, 1876.

97 "The Great Gale – Loss of Life at Montauk Point," *Brooklyn Daily Eagle*, December 18, 1876.

98 *Annual Report of the Operations of the United States Life-Saving Service for the Fiscal Year Ending June 30, 1877* (Washington: Government Printing Office, 1877), 17.

99 Rattray, 124.

100 Journal kept at Ditch Plain, Montauk Station, Dec. 1, 1873 – Feb. 8, 1878.

101 "Brig Ashore at Montauk," *Corrector*, September 8, 1877.

Chapter 7 – Notable Shipwrecks 1878-1914

102 "The Hattie V. Kelsey," *Sag Harbor Express*, September 12, 1878.

103 *Annual Report of the United States Life-Saving Service for the Fiscal Year Ended June 30, 1882* (Washington: Government Printing Office, 1883), 175.

104 Untitled, *East Hampton Star*, August 25, 1888.

105 "The Wrecked Steamship," *East Hampton Star*, January 19, 1889.

106 Rattray, 133.

107 "Historic Long Island; Salvagers of 1889," *Suffolk County News*, August 27, 1959.

108 Rattray, 133-134.

109 Sherrill Foster, "Two Shipwrecks." In *Revealing the Past: the Historical Works Regarding East Hampton, New York of Norton Daniels, Sherrill Foster, Mac Griswold, and Hugh King,"* Tom Twomey (ed). (Bridgehampton: East End Press, 2014), 348.

110 Rattray, 141.

111 "Wrecked on Montauk," *Sag Harbor Express,* February 23, 1893.

112 Ibid.

113 Ibid.

114 "Town Talk," *Suffolk County News,* July 28, 1899.

115 "Schooner Ashore," *Brooklyn Daily Eagle,* September 6, 1903.

116 "Schooner in Distress," *East Hampton Star,* March 10, 1905.

117 Rattray, 158.

118 "Destroy Wreck of Buena Ventura," *New York Tribune,* December 17, 1906.

119 "Life Savers to the Rescue," *New York Times,* February 5, 1908.

120 *The Master Mate and Pilot,* (New York: American Association of Masters, Mates and Pilots, June 1908), p. 252.

121 "Watermelons Galore," *Brooklyn Daily Eagle,* June 27, 1908.

122 "Beach Burning Ship; Passengers Asleep," *New York Times,* April 8, 1912.

123 Ibid.

124 "Steamer is Run on Rocks because of Fire in Hold," *Binghamton Press,* April 8, 1912.

125 Ibid.

126 "Blazing Ontario Left to Her Fate," *New York Times,* April 10, 1912.

127 *Annual Report of the United States Life-Saving Service for the Fiscal Year Ended June 30, 1912* (Washington: Government Printing Office, 1913), 84-85.

128 "Ontario a Total Loss," *New York Sun,* April 11, 1912.

129 Sheard, 94.

Chapter 8 – Notable Shipwrecks 1915-2000s

130 Rattray, 176.

131 "Schooner Loaded with Whiskey Wrecked," *County Review,* January 5, 1923.

132 "Madonna V is a Complete Wreck," *East Hampton Star,* January 5, 1923.

133 "Loaded Fishing Steamer Osprey Runs Aground Near Montauk Point," *East Hampton Star,* September 13, 1929.

134 "Heroic Crew Sticks to Stranded Steamer on Rocks off Montauk," *Brooklyn Daily Eagle,* November 18, 1930.

135 "Fog Dims Seaboard; Three Ships Aground," *New York Times,* November 18, 1930.

136 Osmers, Henry, *Living on the Edge: Life at the Montauk Point Lighthouse 1930-1945* (Denver: Outskirts Press, 2009), 75.

137 "Canadian Boat Algie, Beached at Montauk with 3550 Cases," *East Hampton Star,* February 20, 1931.

138 Ibid.

139 "Yacht Grounds Near Montauk; 5 Saved in Dory, *New York Herald Tribune,* June 30, 1934.

140 "Shipwrecked Skipper at Montauk Blames Women for His Bad Luck," *East Hampton Star,* July 5, 1934.

141 "Boat Strikes Reef off Montauk," *The Watchman,* August 2, 1934.

142 "Montauk," *East Hampton Star,* August 2, 1934.
143 "Fishing Boat Goes Aground with 40 Aboard," *East Hampton Star,* July 4, 1935.
144 Osmers, *Living on the Edge: Life at the Montauk Point Lighthouse 1930-1945,* 75.
145 Superintendent J. T. Yates to Commissioner of Lighthouses, July 20, 1935. Correspondence of the Bureau of Lighthouses 1911-1939. Box 1004, E50, File 1546. National Archives, Record Group 26.
146 "Tanker Hauled Off; No Fish Damage," *Patchogue Advance,* July 26, 1935.
147 Ibid.
148 "Montauk," *East Hampton Star,* July 18, 1935.
149 "Tugs Free Oil Tanker Grounded off Montauk," *New York Herald Tribune,* July 21, 1935.
150 "Sun Tanker Moved off Montauk Rocks on Saturday," *East Hampton Star,* July 25, 1935.
151 "Trawler Amelia D Raised by Merritt, Chapman, Scott," *East Hampton Star,* September 5, 1935.
152 "Men Fish for Swordfish; Fish Lose Hearty Catch," *Mid-Island Mail,* July 13, 1938.
153 Ernest S. Clowes, *The Hurricane of 1938 on Eastern Long Island,* Bridgehampton: Hampton Press, 1939), 18-19.
154 "Loss of 6 Men on 'Ocean View' Told by Survivors of Steamer," *East Hampton Star,* September 29, 1938.
155 "Submarine Rescues 18 off Long Island, Party Adrift 33 Hours," *New York Times,* September 4, 1945.
156 "Save All Aboard as Party Boat Founders Near Montauk Point," *Newsday,* August 18, 1947.
157 Ibid.
158 "No Warning; Mate Tells How Boat Capsized," *Utica Daily Press,* September 3, 1951.
159 Ibid.
160 Tom Clavin, *Dark Noon; the Final Voyage of the Fishing Boat "Pelican,"* (New York: International Marine-McGraw Hill, 2005), 141.
161 Ibid, 142.
162 Ibid, 213.
163 Ibid, 213-214.
164 "Survivors Tell Hearing Boat was Overloaded," *East Hampton Star,* September 6, 1951.
165 "Fifth Man Denies Panic on Pelican," *New York Times,* September 7, 1951.
166 "The Pelican Disaster is Closed by Coroner," *New York Times,* November 30, 1951.
167 "A Trip of Terror; Each Labor Day Brings Memories of Pelican Disaster," *Newsday,* September 2, 2001.
168 Clavin, 221.
169 "Boat Overturns, Angler Drowned," *Suffolk County News,* October 16, 1953.
170 "Boat Overturns in Heavy Seas; Man Missing," *East Hampton Star,* October 15, 1953.
171 "1 Lost, 5 Rescued as Fishing Boat Overturns in Ocean," *Newsday,* October 12, 1953.
172 "Fire Destroys Scamp," *Patchogue Advance,* August 22, 1957.
173 "Fire Ruins Boat Used in Sea Trip," *Newsday,* August 15, 1957.
174 "Trawler Sinks Offshore at Montauk," *East Hampton Star,* May 14, 1959.
175 "Destroyer Salvage Operations Continue at Montauk in Effort to Save Baldwin," *East Hampton Star,* April 27, 1961.
176 "52 Rescued off L.I. as Fishing Boat, Hit by Trawler, Sinks," *New York Times,* August 30, 1961.
177 "LI Boat Crashes, Sinks; Rescue 54," *Newsday,* August 29, 1961.
178 "All Safe as Party Boat Joshua B Sinks," *East Hampton Star,* August 31, 1961.
179 "Blame R. I. Skipper in Collision," *Newsday,* September 6, 1961.
180 "Three Make Shore as Boat Capsizes at Montauk Point," *East Hampton Star,* October 17, 1963.

181 Ibid.
182 "Fear 5 Drowned off Montauk," *Newsday*, August 21, 1967.
183 Ibid.
184 "Yawl Wrecked at Point," *East Hampton Star*, May 11, 1978.
185 "Yawl Still Aground," *East Hampton Star*, May 18, 1978.
186 "The Day Amazon Went Aground in Montauk," *East Hampton Star*, May 2, 2013.
187 "Vessel is Wrecked at Montauk," *East Hampton Star*, December 20, 1979.
188 Ibid.
189 Ibid.
190 "Lobster Boat Aground," *East Hampton Star*, April 29, 1982.
191 Ibid.
192 "Search for Windblown Turns up Wreckage, but Four Still Missing," *Suffolk Life*, April 4, 1984.
193 Ibid.
194 "2 Montauk Fishermen Lost at Sea," *Newsday*, March 5, 1993.
195 "Search for Montauk Crew Suspended," *Newsday*, March 6, 1993.
196 "Miracle at Sea; the Heroic Rescue of Montauk Fisherman John Aldridge," *Dan's Papers*, August 2, 2013.
197 "Missing Montauk Fisherman Rescued," *East Hampton Star*, July 25, 2013.
198 "Montauk Lobsterman used Rubber Boots to Keep Afloat While Lost 12 Hours at Sea," *New York Daily News*, July 25, 2013.
199 "Coast Guard Honored for Ocean Rescue of Montauk Lobsterman," *Dan's Papers*, December 20, 2013.

Chapter 9 – Lost at Sea Memorial

200 "Interview with Malcolm Frazier," *Newsday*, September 16, 1996.
201 "Honoring Fishermen Lost at Sea," *New York Daily News*, October 11, 1999.
202 "Finding the Unknown Fishermen," *Newsday*, February 13, 1999.
203 "Shrine Nearer for Lost Seamen," *New York Daily News*, May 19, 1999.
204 "Honoring Fishermen Lost at Sea," *New York Daily News*, October 11, 1999.
205 "Records of Rev. Nathaniel Huntting."

Index

Aldridge, John	143
Amagansett Life Saving Station	1, 58
Amsterdam State Park	93
Baker, Thomas	78
Baker, William L.	60
Beebe, Frederick C.	10
Beebe-McLellan surfboat	10, 11
Behan, John	130
Behan, Lester	134, 135
Bennett, Charles Raynor	17
Bennett, David H.	60
Bennett, Elijah M.	24
Bennett, Pulaski	46
Benson, Frank Sherman	106
Best, Eric	74
Bistrian Sand and Gravel Corporation	138
Blue Anchor Society	7
Blunt, Edmund March	2
Blunt, George William	2
Bock, Margaret Buckridge	119
Breeches buoy	13
Bruckenthal, Nathan B.	74
Buckridge, Thomas	119, 122
Camp Wikoff	32, 46
Carroll, Edward	128, 129, 130
Carroll, Howard	129
Church Estate	123
"The Churches," Montauk	136
Clark, Scott	141
Collins, Robert	60
Conklin, Theodore	100
Conkling Jr., Jeremiah	146

Connick, David	141
Coston, Martha	11-12
Coston signal	11-12
Covert, James W.	5-6
Culloden Point, Montauk	78, 107, 123, 125
Curles, Purnell	130, 131
Davis, Walter H.	114
Dead Man's Cove, Montauk	138
Dering, Henry Packer	81
Dickinson, Phineas	46
Ditch Plain Coast Guard Station	34, 35, 36-37, 48, 49, 89, 118, 119
Ditch Plain Life Saving Station	2, 5, 31-50, 84, 93, 94, 95, 97, 100, 102, 103, 106, 108, 110, 111, 114, 115, 122, 123, 124
Dominy, Arthur	20, 46
Dominy, Nathaniel	17, 107
Donovan, Roberta Gosman	146
Driscoll, Paul	141
Duryea, Perry B.	123, 129
Edwards, Albert	94
Edwards, Gabriel	59
Edwards, Jesse	56, 58
Edwards, Joshua	37-38, 59
Endeavor Shoals, Montauk	89
False Point, Montauk	135
Faunce, John	3, 4
Filer, George E.	56-57
First House, Montauk	ix, xi
Fishangri-La, Montauk	128
Forsberg, Carl	129, 136
Fort Pond Bay, Montauk	78, 100, 107, 108, 123, 124, 125, 127, 128, 133, 137, 139
Foster, Sherrill	104
Francis, Joseph	9, 10
Francis surfboat	10
Frazier, Malcolm	145
Fresnel, Augustin	3
Garfield, Lucretia Rudolph	7, 8
Georgica Coast Guard Station	69
Georgica Life Saving Station	16

INDEX

Gin Beach, Montauk	99
Gish, Noel	21
Gould, Patrick	37, 83
Grimes, Vincent	129
Halsey, Albert	94
Halsey, William Donaldson	86-87
Hamilton, Alexander	1, 2
Hand, James Howard	16
Harlow, Jetur Reeve	59
Hawley, William	59
Hedges, Carl H.	39, 110, 111, 112, 113, 114, 115, 116
Hedges, Henry P.	81-82
Hewitt, George	131
Hither Hills State Park	136
Hither Plain Coast Guard Station	51-53, 57, 58, 59, 64, 66, 67, 69,
Hither Plain Life Saving Station	2, 5, 6, 51-67, 94, 99-100, 103, 106, 108, 114, 119
Hobart, John	37
Hodnik, Anne	146
Hodnik, Joseph	142, 146
Hone, Harold	118
Humane Society of Massachusetts	1
Huntington, Abel	87
Huntting, Henry E.	6, 18, 19, 23, 24, 37-38, 56
Hurricane of 1938	34, 53, 125
Iceboat	14
Jones, Archie	129
Jones Bar, Montauk	130
Jones Reef, Montauk	108, 135
Keepers (of life saving stations)	4, 14, 18, 19
Kimball, Sumner Increase	3, 4, 6, 7, 8, 9, 14, 117
King, Egbert	46, 60
King, Everett	119
King, Hiram Francis	59, 69
King, Tommie	133
Lanman, Charles	ix, 84
Lawrence, John B.	53
Leo, Arnold	145
Lesnikowski, Tovey	146

Lester, George	89
Life-Saving Benevolent Association	23
Life-Saving Benevolent Association of New York	1, 37, 84
Light-House Board	3
Lockwood, Pat	146
Loper, Abram	6
Loper, Oliver L.	47
Lost at Sea Memorial	94, 125, 130, 142, 145-148
Lyle, David A.	12
Lyle gun	12
Manning, Daniel	31
McLellan, Charles H.	10
Meade, Joseph	69
Mecox Life Saving Station	95
Mershon, Stephen	85-86
Miller, Anna	20
Miller, Arthur	51, 60
Miller, Charles	32
Miller, Charles F.	59
Miller, Charles S.	46
Miller, David	114
Miller, David H.	46, 47-48, 60
Miller, Jack	117
Miller, John E.	114
Miller, Jonathan A.	24, 25
Miller, Russell Garfield	39
Miller, William B.	39, 60
Monomoy surfboat	11
Montauk Association	34
Montauk Fire Department	126, 136, 139
Montauk Historical Society	145
Montauk Point Life Saving Station	5, 23-29
Montauk Point Lighthouse	ix, 2, 23, 29, 37, 77, 81, 89, 93, 108, 109, 117, 122, 125, 135, 141, 145
Montauk Point Lighthouse Museum	92
Montauk Yacht Club	132
Mulford, Lewis	146
Mulford, Thomas Jefferson	85
Mundus, Frank	129
Napeague Coast Guard Station	69, 70-74, 117
Napeague Life Saving Station	4, 94, 99, 107

INDEX

New York Ocean Science Laboratory	137, 139
Newell, William A.	1
Odin, John M.	42
O'Neil, Charles W.	42
Osborn, Alexander	94
Osborne, George H.	53-54, 56, 99
Overton, Jacqueline	3
Oyster Cove, Montauk	109
Parsons, Henry	146
Parsons, Maria D.	21
Parsons, William D.	57, 58, 107, 115
Payne, Jonathan	6
Pike, Earl M.	42, 59, 124
Point Wells (Coast Guard cutter)	74, 138, 141
Ponquogue Lighthouse	(see Shinnecock Lighthouse)
Preparatory Long Distance Signal	18
Prohibition	39, 117
Promised Land	115, 116, 120, 125
Pupo, Nicholas	142
Race Point surfboat	10
Rattray, Jeannette Edwards	15, 78, 92, 95, 104, 106, 107, 110, 118
Raymond, William	10
Raymond surfboat	10
Reeves, Henry A.	18, 19
Remington, August E.	53-54, 56
Revenue Cutter Service	1, 2, 9
Revenue Marine	1
Ripley, Thomas	23
Ripley (Coast Guard cutter)	74
Sabo, Edmund	142
Samuelson, Gary	139
Scanlon, Robert	128, 130
Schellinger, Abraham	78
Schellinger, Jr., William	146
Scott, James G.	101, 102, 108, 110
Scribner, Seth	125
Sears, George	48
Second House, Montauk	ix, xi, 99
Shadmoor State Park	85, 86
Shagwong Buoy	132

Shagwong Reef	78, 81, 100, 106, 120, 125
Sheard, Bradley	115
Shinnecock Lighthouse	86-87, 89
Ships	
A L Hardy	89
A V H	108
Algie	119-120
Amazon	138
Amelia D	123-124
Amsterdam	93
Anna Mary	143
Anne Louise	142, 146
Annie L Wilcox	120-121
Argus	108
Atlantic Cape	137
Augustus Hunt	39
U.S.S. Baldwin	133-134
Buena Ventura	109-110
Calypso	139
Chippewa	111-113
Circassian	95-97
Coastwise	108
Comanche	119
Comanche II	121-122
Cuba	109
HMS Culloden	78-80
Dragnet	138
Edna	124
Edward Quesnel	81-82
Elizabeth R	139-140
Ella May	108
Elsie Fay	106
Emma	89
Exception	109
Fannie	108
Fannie J Bartlett	107
Favorite	103
Felicite	135
Flying Cloud	37, 83-84

INDEX

Freda M	130
Friendship	80
George Appold	103-105,115
George Curtis	116
George M Grant	113
Great Eastern	89-92
Harry Bowen	119
Hattie V Kelsey	99
Idalia	97
Jennie Lee	93-94
Johanna Lenore	142
John & Lucy	77-78
John D Buckalew	99-100
John Milton	85-88
Joseph	106
Joshua B	134-135
Julia (1848)	82
Julia (1935)	124
Lewis A King	102-103
Ligera	81
Lizzie M Dean	100
Lucy Morgan	100
Madonna V	117-118
Marcellus	82
Margaret Mary	143
Marpo V	127-128
Mary	78
Mary A	107
Mary Milnes	93
Mary P Mosquito	124
Matanzas	110
Mavis	120
Merganser	92
Mike Ahoy	130-131
Minnie	140
Montrose	94-95
Nantucket Lightship #11	82-83

Ocean View	125
Olga	82
Ontario	113-116
Oriole	107
Orion	81
Osprey	118
Peggy	80
Pelican	128-130
Pendleton's Satisfaction	109
Petrel	119
Plato	82
Princess	126
Raritan Sun	122-123
Red Sail	126-127, 133
Ricky E	135
Ripple	132
Rose W	128
Ruth R	125
Sand Bay	126
Scamp	132
Serena	142
Shamrock	108
Sophie G	140-141
Sojourn	136
Stormy Weather	137
Susan	81
Tacoma	125
Tattler	119
Thomas R Woolley	117
Triumph	81
Undine	132-133
Unnamed vessel (1955)	131
Unnamed vessel (1967)	136
Viking Star	136, 141
William Faxson	93
Wind Blown	141-142
Winifred	110-111

Smith, Knowles	39
Sosinski, Anthony	143
Southwest Ledge buoy	134
Starrin, Lloyd	42
Stedman, Michael	141
Stratton, Frank S.	32, 38, 100, 103
Stratton, Samuel T.	31, 37
Statton, Theodore	57-58
Terbell, Jason	84
Third House	ix, xii, 37, 84, 100
Turtle Cove, Montauk	23, 108, 130, 133, 135
Tuthill, Craig	139
Uihlein, Henry	136
United States Coast Guard	6, 9, 69, 116, 117
United States Coast Guard Station Montauk	37, 69-75, 135, 137, 138, 139, 141, 143
United States Life-Saving Service	5, 7, 99, 117
Vaughan, Carl	48
Vigilant, Michael	141
Walter, Jason	143
Warner, Frank D.	39, 42, 43, 118, 120
Warrington, George	122
Watch Hill Life Saving Station	114
Wessells, Cecil F.	59
White, Dick	145
Women's National Relief Association	7, 100, 103